Visitor's Guide
GRAN CANARIA

Gran Canaria

Page 138-9

Page 106-7

Las Palmas

Arucas

Puerto de las Nieves

Teror

Puerto de la Aldea

Telde

Puerto de Mogán

Puerto Rico

Page 59

Page 91

Playa del Inglés

Page 71

Page 34-5

N
W   E
S

VISITOR'S GUIDE
GRAN CANARIA

Christopher Turner

MPC®
HUNTER

Published by:
Moorland Publishing Co Ltd,
Moor Farm Road West, Ashbourne,
Derbyshire DE6 1HD England

ISBN 0 86190 514 8

Published in the USA by:
Hunter Publishing Inc,
300 Raritan Center Parkway, CN 94, Edison, NJ 08818

British Library Cataloguing in Publication Data:
A catalogue record for this book is available from the British Library.

Colour origination by: Reed Reprographics, Ipswich

Printed in Hong Kong by: Wing King Tong Co Ltd

Front cover: Puerto de Mogán (Chris Turner)
Rear cover: Hibiscus (MPC Picture Collection)
page 3: Playa del Inglés (MPC Picture Collection)

Illustrations have been supplied by:
Chris Turner: pages 11 (bottom), 15 (top), 19, 22, 46 (botom), 50, 51, 55, 63 (top), 70, 79,
102, 103, 110, 111, 115, 118, 123, 126, 127, 142, 150, 155, 162. All the remaining
illustrations are from the MPC Picture Collection.

MPC Production Team:
Editorial & Design: John Robey
Cartography: Mick Usher

While every care has been taken to ensure that the information in this
book is as accurate as possible at the time of publication, the publisher
and authors accept no responsibility for any loss, injury or inconven-
ience sustained by anyone using this book.

CONTENTS

Symbols

π Archaeological Site ⬧ Water Sports/Boat Trips

🏰 Castle/Fortification ⓘ Tourist Information

🏢 Building of Interest ＊ Other Place of Interest

🏛 Museum/Art Gallery ❀ Garden

♦ Church ➤ Birdlife

🚶 Walking ⏇ Beach

🐑 Nature Wildlife ⚑ Beautiful View/Natural
Reserve Phenomenon

Topography

🌊 Lakes ▣ Town

⛰ Mountain Range ┃ Major Road

〰 Rivers ● Village

┆ Minor Road

How To Use This Guide

This MPC Visitor's Guide has been designed to be as easy to use as possible. Each chapter covers a region or itinerary in a natural progression which gives all the background information to help you enjoy your visit. MPC's distinctive margin symbols, the important places printed in bold, and a comprehensive index enable the reader to find the most interesting places to visit with ease.

At the end of each chapter an Additional Information section gives specific details such as addresses and opening times, making this guide a complete sightseeing companion.

At the back of the guide the Fact File, arranged in alphabetical order, gives practical information and useful tips to help you plan your holiday before you go and while you are there.

The maps of each region show the main towns, villages, roads, and places of interest, but are not designed as route maps and motorists should always use a good recommended road atlas.

Introduction

Although the Mediterranean resorts are often promoted as winter-sun holiday destinations, the winter rainfall of most usually exceeds considerably that of the south coast of England. But by flying due south for less than one hour longer, often at no greater cost, the chill north winds will at last have petered out, and a warm sun will be shining virtually without interruption. The Canary Islands, 'The Fortunate Isles', have been reached.

However, the Canaries are far from being just a winter holiday destination. In mid-summer, when their temperatures are only moderately higher, the climate is, once again, nigh perfect: the scorching heat of the Mediterranean will never be approached.

Those who select Gran Canaria for their holiday destination from the other islands in the group are chiefly attracted by its golden sand beaches (which include the famous Sahara-style sand dunes of Maspalomas), its dramatic mountains, the idyllic pastoral scenery of the island's north, and the fascinating, cosmopolitan city of Las Palmas.

Some visitors will spend most of their holiday relaxing on a sandy beach, perhaps only leaving it during the day to purchase duty-free drinks, tobacco and electronic goods in Gran Canaria's irresistible shops. Others will prefer to make excursions to other parts of this beautiful island. *Visitor's Guide: Gran Canaria* provides invaluable assistance to both categories. For the first time, each resort is explored in depth: not one of them is ideal for everybody but, conversely, very few holidaymakers will have difficulty in chosing a location on the island that suits them perfectly.

Although many itineraries are described in great detail, with all the roads identified, not everyone will have a car at all times, therefore appropriate bus information, which includes the numbers of the routes and their connections, is also provided.

The aim of this book is to ensure that you make the utmost of your Gran Canaria holiday, whenever you go, wherever you stay and whatever your interests. It will prove to be a tremendous time and money saver.

Geography, Fauna & Flora

Gran Canaria is one of seven islands that, accompanied by six tiny islets, make up the Canary Islands (Islas Canarias), renowned since ancient times for their benign all-year round climate. Probably to overcome this, unlucky number of 13, another island has been 'sighted' on the horizon from time to time, and even named — San Borondon. Volcanic in origin, the islands form an archipelago lying just off Morocco's Atlantic coastline, approximately 320 miles north of the Tropic of Cancer. From west to east, they comprise: El Hierro, La Palma, La Gomera, Tenerife, Gran Canaria, Lanzarote and Fuerteventura.

Although the Canaries are on the same latitude as much of Florida, 32-33°, the debilitating summer heat and humidity of

previous page: Cruz de Tejeda in the central mountains of Gran Canaria, the island's most popular inland excursion

the American state is never approached, due to the cold Canary current, which flows to the islands from the north Atlantic.

Gran Canaria, Fuerteventura and Lanzarote together form a province of Spain and are administered from Las Palmas. Las Palmas, situated in the north-east corner of Gran Canaria, has a population of 40,000, and is the eighth largest city in Spain;it is also the most important city in the Canaries, from a commercial and historical viewpoint; its location on this island primarily distinguishes Gran Canaria from the others in the group.

Most foreign (ie non-Spanish) tourists who spend a holiday in Gran Canaria arrive between November and February, to escape the cold and dark of the northern winters. Virtually all of them now stay on the south coast of the island, where the sun shines more reliably than further north. However, due to its low rainfall, the countryside immediately behind this coast is predominantly arid, giving no hint of the verdant, paradisical scenery further north.

Gran Canaria, an almost circular island, the third largest in the group, covers an area of 1,532 sq km. Apart from a short interruption at the western extremity, a main road follows its entire coastline, which enthusiastic motorists can therefore see in just one day. Expeditions to the interior, however, take much longer: roads zig-zag, climb and descend, and what appears from the map to involve a reasonably short journey can take up much of the day. Nevertheless, those who forego visiting the north and centre of Gran Canaria will be missing the very essence of the island: craggy mountain peaks towering over slender eucalyptus trees, exuberant palms, prickly cacti and lush orchards, and everywhere, and at all seasons, bougainvillaea, with its brilliant red, purple, white and orange blossom enlivening the white walls of pastoral cottages.

Approximately 2,000 species of plants and 200 of birds have been identified on Gran Canaria, some of them unique to the archipelago. Canary Pines and Canary Palms are varieties found nowhere else, but the most spectacular 'tree' is undoubtedly a strange survivor from the earth's Tertiary Period, the dragon tree (*dracaneo draco*), examples of which have lived for several thousand years. The name derives from the spiky, fierce appearance of the tree, not its blood-red sap, as some assert. Techni-

Gran Canaria's dramatic volcanic mountains (above) contrast with the sandy beaches of the southern resorts (below)

*The morning's catch left
to dry in the sun*

*These coconut palms on
the beach at St Agustín
are a rare sight on Gran
Canaria*

cally, it is more a plant than a tree, as it lacks a solid trunk, soft fibres rather than wood growing within the bark. The early inhabitants believed that coughs could be cured by drinking its sap. Dragon trees also survive in Madeira, while a superb example thrives in the front garden of a private school behind the French Consulate at Tangier, Morocco — almost certainly the most northerly example.

Apart from the ubiquitous bougainvillaea, most flowers will be familiar to north European holidaymakers, although some of them only as pot plants. Particularly impressive is the poinsettia, bushes of which grow wild along the roadsides to a great height — some pot plant! A flower which cannot be grown in Europe, but which has come to represent the Canaries' flora, is the *strelitzia*, better known as the Bird of Paradise flower. Many tourists return home clutching bunches of this yellow and purple flower, which they have bought at the last moment: the waxy blooms have an unusually long life. As may be expected, cacti thrive in the dry south, some species being unique to the islands.

The fauna of Gran Canaria is less spectacular than its flora, even the plentiful rabbits and lizards rarely appearing for tourists. Birds of prey are only usually spied in the mountains; they may include white eagles, buzzards and hawks, all of which hunt smaller birds. Bird enthusiasts will seek in vain for bright-yellow canaries (named from the islands rather than the other way round) flying free, as the natural colouring of this bird is primarily brown, with just a few yellow streaks. Only in captivity do all its feathers turn yellow, and only the male bird sings.

Due to the equable climate of the Canaries, most birds stay throughout the year, and their flying ability, in consequence, has become very restricted. In spring and autumn, local birds are augmented by migrating strangers on route to and from the north.

The waters around the Canaries are well stocked with fish, but species are rather limited. Most numerous are tuna, mackerel, sardines and swordfish, plus several local varieties: including cherne and vieja. Shellfish is almost non-existent, only small shrimps, winkles and limpets finding these coasts to their liking.

None of the Canary crops is indigenous to the islands, each being a post-colonization introduction. The Roman historian

Pliny referred to date palms and olives, but many centuries were to pass before sugar cane, vines, mangoes, papayas, potatoes, yams, avocados, tomatoes and bananas were introduced. Tomatoes are now by far the most important export crop, followed by cucumbers, aubergines and onions. The price of locally-grown bananas, which are exceptionally tasty, is now undercut by third-world countries, thereby making them uneconomic to grow commercially. Almonds, roses and carnations remain profitable exports, as do the delicious, tiny Canary potatoes, although production is limited, most of it going to Spain. Some wine is still produced, but only sufficient for local consumption. Game birds are plentiful and, during the season, August-December, they may be found on the menus of the more expensive restaurants.

Gran Canaria, of course, is small, and much of it very dry, with erosion, even in the fertile areas, creating a shallow depth of soil. Desalination plants have virtually solved the island's former water supply problem, but irrigation is essential for the farmer, and the streams are therefore ducted: due to this, the ravines (*barrancos*) in the south, where there is little rainfall to water their slopes, have aquired an exceptionally arid appearance. It will be seen that the mountain slopes are terraced to the highest level possible. so that maximum use is made of the land available. Fortunately, the soil is volcanic and extremely fertile.

Climate

The Canary Islands' moderate temperatures are their greatest attraction; almost never, at least at lower levels, will the visitor feel cold; and rarely will temperatures exceed 85°F. Rainfall is light, almost negligible in the south, most of it usually occuring between mid-November and mid-March. Sunshine, however, is rather less predictable; September, October and March being generallly, but not always, the sunniest months. Annoyingly, in the south, midwinter, when most visit the island, is often the cloudiest period. To emphasize that the climate of Gran Canaria is not entirely predictable, the November to mid-March period in 1994/5 was completely dry, rainfall occurring from mid-March to mid-April.

Hibiscus and bourgainvillaea add a bright splash of colour to the Canary Islands

Poinsettia, grown as a tender pot plant in northern Europe, thrives as a large bush on Gran Canaria

Cacti enjoy the warm dry climate of Gran Canaria

There are dramatic differences in the sunshine figures for Puerto Rico and Las Palmas, the former resort, together with Puerto de Mogan, being the sunniest on the island. It is said that the international airport usually marks the break between the sunny and the cloudy regions. Climate statistics for Gran Canaria are measured at the airport, and do not accurately represent the situation at either Las Palmas or the southern resorts. When, on occasions, the wind blows from the south-west rather than the usual north-east, everything can change, with the north having clearer weather. A south-east sirocco wind from the Sahara blows usually twice a year, bearing with it desert sand. This is most unpleasant, the sky becomes yellow and the sun all but disappears; those with weak chests are advised to stay indoors to avoid the choking air. Fortunately, the sirocco rarely blows for more than three days.

Las Palmas lies in a bowl, surrounded by mountains, and air pollution is a great problem during the summer, when a heavy, Los Angeles-type smog, known as *panza de burro* (donkey's stomach), hangs over the city, blotting out the sun. July and August are definately the worst months for a Las Palmas holiday.

At any time of the year, visitors are advised to take warm clothing with them when visiting the high mountains, which reach a height of 1,949m (6,393ft) at the summit of Pico de las Nieves, and are frequently cloudy. Even on the coast during the winter months a jacket or sweater may well be needed from early evening until mid morning, particularly if a wind is blowing.

History

Because the Canary Islands, although located more than 1,000km (600 miles) from the Iberian peninsula, have long been an integral part of Spain, their history since the late fifteenth century incorporates that of the entire country. However, in this book only events specific to Gran Canaria are outlined.

A surprise to many is that the Canary Islands, adjacent to the African coast, are classed officially as part of Europe, indeed they are within the European Union (but not for Customs purposes).

MYTHS & EARLY HISTORY

It is believed that the Canary Islands arose from the sea bed as part of volcanic activity 140 million years ago. Whether or not they at one time formed part of the 'lost continent' of Atlantis, referred to by the Greek philosopher Plato, is a matter of debate, and it seems unlikely that the question will ever be conclusively answered. Others believe that they provided the inspiration for the Garden of the Hesperides (Herodotus) and the Elysian Fields (Homer). However, the first certain reference to the archipelago was by Pliny the Elder (AD23-79), who recorded an expedition to it by King Juba of Mauretania in AD30. Puzzlingly, he refers to the ruins of great buildings, and a complete lack of inhabitants apart from large dogs (*canis* in Latin, and the source of the Canaries' name), two of which were captured. It was also Pliny who first dubbed the group 'The Fortunate Isles'. Gran Canaria had several earlier names, including *Tamaran* (Brave Men) and Paradise of Birds.

THE GUANCHES

In spite of Pliny's description of uninhabited islands — possibly the natives were in hiding — Arab merchants appear to have traded with Gran Canaria around 1000AD. The people that they would have traded with are known as Guanches, a Canary word derived from *guan* (men) and *achinech* (white mountain), an obvious reference to Tenerife's snow-clad Mount Teide. Only the natives of Tenerife were originally called Guanches, but eventually the name was applied to all the aboriginal islanders. Who were these people, and where did they come from? Many of them are known to have had fair hair and pale eyes, leading anthropologists to suggest a Scandinavian origin. However, it has been pointed out that some Berbers from the North-African mountains possess similar features, and their close proximity to the islands makes them more probable candidates.

The Guanches have long been extinct as an identifiable race, although inter-breeding with their Spanish conquerors obviously occurred. What is known is that the Guanches lived a Neolithic, stone-age exisitence, which had advanced little over the centuries. They could not write, nor were they navigators, little contact being made between the inhabitants of the various islands in spite of the short distances that separated them. The Guanches lived primarily in caves, some of which still retain evidence of their occupancy, kept goats and pigs, and operated a primitive form of agriculture dependant on maize for grinding into a flour that is still known as *gofio*.

Originally, there were ten Guanche tribes on the island, each with a chief, who appointed separate advisers on secular and religious matters. Eventually, Andamanar, wife of Gumidafe, based on Gáldar, united the tribes, and her Guanarteme dynasty then ruled Gran Canaria until the Spanish annexed the island.

REDISCOVERY

Strangely, the existence of the Canaries seems to have been forgotten, at least by Europeans, until the Genoese, Lancellotto Mallocello, 'rediscovered' them early in the fourteenth century. He eventually charted a map of the islands, immodestly naming one of them Lanzarote, after himself. Merchants from Spain, Portugal and Italy now began to trade with the Guanches and, from the information they provided, Angelino Dulcert, a Majorcan cartographer, prepared the first accurate map of the archipelago in 1339.

Trading now continued apace and, in 1342, the island's first bishopric, at Telde, now Gran Canaria's second most important town, was created by Pope Clement VI; friars soon arrived from Majorca, then part of the powerful state of Catalonia, bent on converting the natives to Christianity. No acts of aggression, however, were perpetrated against the inhabitants until, in 1393, Alvaro Becerra, from Seville, carried out sorties to capture Guanches for enslavement in Spain. During one of these, he fearfully witnessed a spectacular eruption of Mount Teide, and dubbed Tenerife 'Hell Island'.

SPANISH COLONIZATION

Enríquez III of Castile gave the order for Spanish colonization of the Canary Islands to begin in 1402, commissioning Jean de

opposite: Casa de Colón in Las Palmas is one of the architectural legacies of the Spanish colonization of the Canary Islands, and where Columbus is believed to have stayed

Bethencourt, a Norman baron, to take, in the name of Christianity, the least populated islands: Lanzarote, Fuerteventura, La Gomera and El Hierro. In spite of their primitive weapons, the Guanches, aided by the mountainous terrain, offered stiff opposition, and it was not until 1496 that the largest island, Tenerife, was finally taken by the Spanish. At one time, the Portuguese also occupied some of the islands for a brief period, but the Treaty of Alcaçovas, in 1480, ended their ambitions in the Canary Islands.

Spaniards invaded Gran Canaria in 1478, Juan Rejón immediately setting up an encampment at Las Palmas. Here again, the Guanches proved strong opponents, and the whole island did not fall until 1483, when Pedro de Vera wiped out the last pockets of resistance. He had been aided by Semidan, a renegade Guanche leader, who was eventually baptized and renamed Fernando.

In a remarkably short space of time, the Guanches completely disappeared as an identifiable race. Many of them had been killed in battle, and some taken into slavery, but the survivors had no resistance against European diseases, which decimated them. Some interbred with their conquerors, and there may still be seen blonde-haired Canarios that betray Guanche ancestry. The initial Spanish encampment at Las Palmas quickly spread eastward across the Guiniguada ravine, which came to serve as a dividing line between the houses of the well-to-do and those of the working classes. El Real de las Palmas was founded on 23 June 1478 and incorporated in the crown of Castile: it was the first city in the Canaries.

An early visitor was Christopher Columbus, who docked at Las Palmas for repairs to be made to his vessels on route to discover America in 1492.

SUGAR & WINE
Sugar cane was introduced to the Canaries from Portuguese-owned Madeira, and sugar became the first major agricultural export from the islands; more than twenty mills were operating in Gran Canaria within fifty years of its annexation. However, the New World's ability to produce cheaper sugar by the mid sixteenth century quickly brought an end to Gran Canaria's all-

important trade. In the long run, this was probably a good thing, as the crop was causing a great deal of soil erosion; in the short term, however, it ruined many of the islanders who, in despair, emigrated to the Americas.

Vines soon took over as the most important crop in Gran Canaria, the sweet malmsey wine produced from them, which is referred to by Shakespeare, being exported primarily to England, in return, chiefly, for wool, there being insufficient pastureland to rear sheep on the islands. Tenerife and Lanzarote, however, were always more important wine producers. Virtually all the small quantity of wine now produced in the Canaries is consumed locally; due to the volcanic soil and strong sunshine, it has a high alcoholic content.

POVERTY TO PROSPERITY

For long, most Canarios belonged to poverty-struck agricultural and fishing communities, only the importance of Santa Cruz de Tenerife and Las Palmas as convenient calling stages for transatlantic merchant ships creating any appreciable income. Peninsular Spain had declined rapidly as a major power since the late sixteenth century, and no investment from the mainland could be expected: the Canaries went into virtual isolation.

An aggressive visitor to the Canaries, in 1797, was Nelson, who attempted to take the strategically-sited port of Santa Cruz de Tenerife for the English; not only did he fail, but he lost an arm in the attempt. The Canary Islands were designated a Spanish province in 1823, but the choice of Santa Cruz de Tenerife as capital gave much annoyance to the inhabitants of Gran Canaria, who felt that Las Palmas should have been selected. A degree of rancour between the old rivals continued until Spain, in 1927, diplomatically divided the Canary Islands into two separate provinces: the western group, still administered from Santa Cruz, and the eastern group, administered from Las Palmas, which has given its name to the province.

Following Napoleon's defeat at Waterloo, and Spain's demise as a combatant nation, many British emigrated to Las Palmas, and soon began to influence the commercial development of the islands. By the mid-nineteenth century, prosperity had brought an end to the isolation of Las Palmas: public buildings were

*A wide variety of fruit and vegetables is grown on Gran Canaria —
harvesting aubergines in the Mogán valley*

*Gran Canaria's balmy climate permits the cultivation of fruits such as
mango and papaya, which are normally only found in the tropics*

Food at the resorts on Gran Canaria is usually designed to suit international tastes, but local dishes can be found — albeit with some difficulty

erected, its enclosing wall demolished and, in 1852, the Canary Islands, as a group, were designated a free port by royal decree.

RAPID NINETEENTH-CENTURY DEVELOPMENT

Fernando León y Castillo, from Telde, Gran Canaria's second largest city, was appointed Spain's Foreign Minister, and became instrumental in the realization of the new port of Las Palmas, known as Puerto de la Luz (Port of Light). The project, engineered by his brother, was an immediate success, and trade quickly outstripped that of its Tenerife rival, Santa Cruz. By the turn of the century, Las Palmas had been adopted by the British navy as its Atlantic base.

Around this time, two important crops were introduced to the Canaries: tomatoes and bananas. The latter was the inspiration of the Englishman, Alfred L. Jones, and his name, under its Spanish adaptation Alfredo, has been given to one of the major streets leading to Las Canteras beach. British companies soon gained a virtual monopoly in the export of both tomatoes and bananas from the Canaries.

THE TWENTIETH CENTURY

World War I, throughout which Spain remained neutral, saw a further upsurge in emigrés from Europe, many of them wealthy refugees, and the already cosmopolitan nature of Las Palmas was consolidated.

It was from Gran Canaria that General Franco, then Captain General of the island's military and civil affairs, unleashed the Spanish Civil War in 1936, but the islands suffered little, compared with peninsular Spain, from the four years of turmoil that followed.

During World War II, Hitler pressurized Franco to permit the German navy to operate a base at Las Palmas in exchange for the promise of eventually presenting him with Gibraltar, but Spain insisted on remaining neutral. Not long after the war ended, Las Palmas, with its constantly warm climate and outstanding beach, evolved into an international tourist resort, and was followed, in the early 1960s, by the development of tourist resorts on the island's sunny south coast. Not everyone prospered, however, and discontent led to 8,000 leaving the Canaries illegally, many of them settling in South America, Venezuela in particular. In the early 1950s, Franco legalized emigration, and a further 150,000 departed from the islands. Franco died in 1975, having appointed Juan Carlos, the present king, as his successor.

Although Spain joined the EEC in 1986, and Gran Canaria, as part of its province of Las Palmas, is therefore a member, it has been permitted to remain outside the EU Customs Union (see Customs and Excise Regulations in the Fact File), and designated a free trade zone. As in the rest of Spain, the world recession of the 1990s has hit the Canary Islands particularly hard and, in 1995, unemployment in Las Palmas had reached approximately 30 per cent. Partly due to this, crimes such as pick-pocketing, mugging and burglary have rocketed, with tourists being prime targets. Extreme care should therefore be taken, and quiet parts of Las Palmas avoided at night. Tourism, however, is steadily increasing, and the reborn fashionability of ocean-liner cruising is a welcome supplement to the income of Puerto de la Luz, the international port of Las Palmas.

Food & Drink

Food lovers are urged, if possible, to book their Gran Canaria hotel on a bed and breakfast basis, otherwise they risk being condemned to tasteless, repetitive 'international' meals, which soon begin to pall. Remember that the hotelier is working on a very tight budget, and also that he wishes to avoid complaints by unsophisticated guests about unfamiliar, 'funny-tasting' dishes. Rarely will he offer anything Spanish, apart, perhaps, from the occasional watery *paella*, and *gazpacho*; local specialities are most certainly out.

Families and younger visitors sometimes opt to interrupt the boredom of hotel meals with the occasional foray to a fast-food outlet, pizzas, pastas, burgers, frankfurters, spit-roasted chickens, and chips (but not fish and chips) being readily available at reasonable prices in all the resorts virtually 24 hours a day. A grade up are restaurants, most of which, like the hotels, serve international dishes, but of a much higher quality; the meat, in particular, is usually excellent, most of the beef and lamb coming from South America.

The South Coast Main Holiday Resorts at a Glance (from East to West)

SAN AGUSTIN
✓ Advantages: small in size, with most accommodation near the beach, relatively select and quiet, attractive promenades.
✗ Disadvantages: can be cloudy, inconvenient for a varied night life and restaurants, step approach to some accommodation.

PLAYA DEL INGLES
✓ Advantages: extensive night life, good selection of restaurants, wide range of accommodation, regular bus services, many shopping/entertainment centres.
✗ Disadvantages: architecturally characterless, lacks an identifiable centre, few trees and no parks, some accommodation is a long walk from the beach, steep access to the beach, excessive time-share and other touting, generally windy afternoons.

MASPALOMAS
Punta de Maspalomas divides the east and west-facing stretches of the south coast.
✓ Adantagess: dramatic sand dunes, luxury hotels, tranquil lagoon.
✗ Disadvantages: isolated situation, strong afternoon winds.

PASITO BLANCO
✓ Advantages: yacht marina, secluded beach, calm sea for divers, good camping site.
✗ Disadvantages: isolated situation, limited shopping, restaurant and entertainment facilities, few hotels.

ARGUINEGUIN

✓ Advantages: Canary atmosphere (rare on the south coast) of an established fishing port, good fish restaurants and *tapas* bars, low prices.

✗ Disadvantages: cement works to the south (but out of view from the north side) unattractive beach, dreary village architecture, no night life.

PATALAVACA

✓ Advantages: pleasant beachfront promenade, well-kept beach.

✗ Disadvantages: consists entirely of beachfront hotels and apartments, limited access to beach from the road, no nightlife outside the hotels.

PUERTO RICO

✓ Advantages: safe golden sand beach, protection from most winds by encompassing hills, verdant parks, restrictions on music volume, game-fishing opportunities.

✗ Disadvantages: long, steep approach to many apartments, little nightlife, limited shopping, isolation, all accommodation is self-catering.

Puerto Rico is dominated by British holidaymakers — to some this is an advantage, to others it is not.

PUERTO DE MOGAN

✓ Advantages: undoubtedly the most architecturally attractive (some say the *only* attractive) development on the coast, vibrant marina, a profusion of flowers, the original port with Canary ambience still survives, highest sunshine record on the coast, boat excursions.

✗ Disadvantages: the most isolated resort, a neglected grey sand beach, no nightlife.

The majority of the highest grade restaurants are those which offer specialities from the Canaries and peninsular Spain — particularly the provinces of Galicia and Asturias, which are renowned for the high quality of their cuisines. These restaurants are naturally the most expensive, but well worth it for the occasional treat. All grades of restaurants in Gran Canaria are, in any case, significantly cheaper than their north European equivalents.

Those who enjoy sampling local dishes, but lack a budget that will stretch to top-class restaurants, are well catered for in peninsular Spain by the ubiquitous *tapas* bars. In these, varying-size portions of regional food may be tried without incurring great expense. Unfortunately, although Gran Canaria is part of Spain, *tapas* bars are far less numerous, particularly at the southern resorts, than in the peninsula, and the variety and quality of their dishes are much lower. The vast majority of holidaymakers, who stay in the south, will find it necessary to make for San Fernando, a 'Spanish' enclave on the north side of the main road and virtually a suburb of Playa del Inglés, in order to track down a genuine *tapas* bar. As may be expected, Las Palmas and the inland towns are much better provided with *tapas* bars. Remember that a *tapas* is a very small, saucer-size portion, while a *ración* is much larger; some dishes are available only in *ración* sizes.

Throughout peninsular Spain, the emphasis in a *tapas* bar is on shellfish, which is virtually non-existent in the waters of the Canary Islands. Imported *gambas* (large prawns) will be deep-frozen and lack the flavour of the fresh version. For this reason, Canarios rarely eat them.

Ethnic restaurants exist in abundance in the resorts, particularly German, Scandinavian, Italian and Chinese; there is also, in Playa del Inglés, an excellent Indonesian restaurant, but Indian restaurants, apart from one each in Las Palmas and San Agustín, are non-existent.

The most commonly served Canary speciality is *papas arrugadas*, 'wrinkled' potatoes, cooked in salted water and served in their jackets with piquant mojo sauce. Others are explained in the Food Vocabulary in the Fact File.

Those who have previously visited Spain will know that Spanish *charcuterie* is delicious, and it may be readily purchased from the larger supermarkets, particularly those in San Fernando and Las Palmas. Ham, chorizo and various types of salami-type meats are economical, tasty fillers for sandwiches, accompanied, perhaps, by sun-ripened tomatoes. Many cheeses, both local and Spanish, are available, although most are rather bland.

While alcoholic drinks are duty-free in the Canaries, virtually all have to be shipped from Europe, and the transportation cost has to be incorporated in the price charged. Nevertheless, it is outrageous that some of the bars and discos in the tourist areas should demand the same prices as in northern Europe. Bars in Las Palmas and inland are much more reasonable, and bottles of alcoholic drinks at most supermarkets are incredibly cheap. A very large gin and tonic (or two) in your room before going out for a meal, followed later by a brandy, will hardly break the bank. In addition to lower prices, the Canary Islands have an advantage over mainland Spain in that foreign drinks are imported from the country of origin, not from Spanish distillers, who invariably produce pale imitations of the same brands. Gordon's gin, for example, comes from London, not Málaga, and the difference in flavour is most noticeable. Transport costs and low duty in Spain, mean that Spanish wine often costs slightly more than on the mainland.

Tap water is drinkable in Gran Canaria, but tastes rather unpleasant. Most will prefer to purchase large bottles of mineral water — gas or non-gas — which is much more palatable, particularly when refrigerated. The local, and most popular brand, is Firgas.

To summarize, Gran Canaria is hardly a gourmet's paradise, but those who make the effort to seek out the limited number of local specialities, which have evolved through Guanche traditions, Spanish tastes and Latin-American influences, are in for a pleasurable, as well as an interesting experience.

Chosing a Resort

Until the early 1960s, visitors to Gran Canaria had little option but to stay in Las Palmas, with its wide range of hotels. Since then, the south coast, due to its much higher sunshine, has gradually become the major tourist destination. It is split into a south-east facing section, dubbed the Costa Canaria, which is entirely built-up and favoured by the Germans, and a south-west facing section, more extensive but less developed, and preferred by the British. Due to the configuration of the mountains and the prevailing north-east wind, less cloud cover can generally be expected the further west the resort is located.

Las Palmas is still preferred by those willing to trade less guaranteed sunshine for a genuine Spanish atmosphere, much lower prices and the superb Las Canteras beach, rated among the most beautiful in the world. Few UK tour operators, however, apart from an occasional city-break specialist, now include this great city in their programme, which virtually excludes it as a centre for British holidaymakers unless they are travelling on a flight-only basis.

In spite of the fact that Gran Canaria's south coast has been developed over a relatively short period, the main resorts possess individual characteristics that vary greatly, and these should be considered before a resort is selected. The entire stretch is linked by buses, but there are no night services along the west-facing coast, and taxis in the Canary Islands are not cheap. The resorts are, of course, dealt with in detail in this book, but the summary on pages 26-7, from east to west, will help first-time visitors to the island make a quick appraisal of each of them, and judge how they meet their own requirements.

The South-East Coast Resorts

1

Canarios claim that the location of Aeropuerto de Gando, Gran Canaria's international airport, frequently marks the island's climatic division — usually cloudy to the north of it, sunny to the south. However, the beaches immediately south of the airport are all of dark volcanic sand and favoured primarily by local families that want to avoid the tourists, sharing them only with the fishermen.

Apart from the old quarter of Las Palmas, the Maspalomas lighthouse, and an occasional defensive tower, there are no vintage buildings of architectural interest to be found along the entire coastline of Gran Canaria: the fishing villages were always poor, and their inhabitants quite unable to afford the splendid balconies and decorated churches that are a feature of the more prosperous inland towns, such as Teror, Telde and Arucas. A similar situation occurs in all the other islands of the archipelago, and those seeking quaint fishing villages overlooking unspoilt beaches of golden sand will be disappointed. Having said this, however, the occasional excursion to a coastal *tapas* bar, where the atmosphere is truly Spanish, provides a refreshing change from the unreality of the tourist resorts (and so are the prices). Those of greatest appeal are indicated throughout this book.

The windy **Bahía de Pozo Izquierdo**, reached by the 14.2 road from the Carretera del Sur at El Doctoral village, is a mecca for both surfboarders and windsurfers. (The map on page 91 covers the area between Bahía de Pozo Izquierdo and San Agustín.)

At **Playa de los Tártagos**, where the dry valley of the Barranco de Tirajana reaches the sea, the coast swings westward and thus faces south-east. Here, the ancient Castillo del Romeral tower overlooks the sea, protecting the fishing village of **La Caleta**, which has a small beach. As has been said, all the beaches on the east coast of Gran Canaria are of dark volcanic sand until Playa del Inglés is reached, but to call them black is inaccurate, as the sands only appear black when they have been lapped by the sea; mid-grey is a more realistic description.

Playa del Cardón, which follows Punta de la Caleta, is much more extensive, ending at Punta de Tradajillo, behind which is based the Aeroclub de Gran Canaria. The club's aeroplanes, which can be seen from the main road, sometimes provide a nasty shock to tourists returning home, as they wrongly think that they are approaching the international airport, desperately grab their baggage and shriek incomprehensibly at the driver to stop the bus.

Immediately south of the Aeroclub, the delightful **Bahía Feliz** opens up, where conditions are ideal for windsurfing, and where championship contests are held. Within this bay, Playa de Trajadillo is an extensive beach, but much of it is gravelly and interspersed with rocks. Finally, before the Costa Canaria proper begins, **Playa del Aguila**, a mixed stone and sand beach appears; this is named after the Cañon del Aguila, another of the many dry ravines that are an important feature of this southern coast.

previous page: Relaxing by the sea at San Agustín

San Agustín

This is where it all began, initially in a quiet way, with a few dignified hotels and improvements to the main beach. As late as 1963, it was possible for a new British pop group called The Beatles, who had already gained a number one in the charts, to spend a quiet holiday at San Agustín undisturbed by fans. Local entrepreneurs learned that northern Europeans were flocking to the Mediterranean coast of Spain to lay on the beaches for most of the day, sizzling in the blazing sun. If their Mediterranean cousins could get rich through such lunacy why not the Canarios, whose sun shone reliably and warmly not just in the summer but throughout the year? It should be appreciated that Las Palmas had become a popular resort earlier, partly *because* of its frequently obscured sun, which assured benign temperatures. Strong sunshine had been considered bad for the health, and a suntan signified that one must be a manual labourer.

Playa de Morro Besudo, almost 200m long, is the most easterly of San Agustín's beaches, but it has a bad reputation as there have been several drownings along parts of it — so it is best avoided by keen swimmers.

Lying back from the west end of the beach is the Centro Commercial Morro Besudo, one of two shopping centres in the town; the bus terminal (29 to Maspalomas and 45 to Palmitos Park) is located in front of it.

Playa de San Agustín, renowned for its crystal clear waters and safe swimming, is the next beach reached, and it was behind this that the town developed. All amenities that might be expected are on offer, including surfboard and pedalo rental. The laying out of the 812 Carretera del Sur road to Las Palmas put a temporary halt to development, but it soon recontinued on the north side of the sunken highway. However, the terrain rises fairly steeply, a fact which should be borne in mind by those booking accommodation in this part of San Agustín. Only a narrow strip of land lies between the *carretera* and the beach until Playa del Inglés is reached; the situation is almost identical with that of Benalmadena on Spain's Costa del Sol. An unusual feature are coconut palms, which can be spotted by those with an eagle eye growing immediately behind the east end of San Agustín beach. There are other locations on the island where

they are also grown, but coconuts, certainly not a usual Canary crop, are a rare sight.

Between the beach and the highway lies the five star Meliá Tamarindos Hotel, incorporating the **Casino Palace Nightclub**, its floorshow regarded as the island's finest. At the casino (jacket and tie obligatory for men) the usual gambling tables will be found, including roulette, blackjack and *chemin de fer*. Passports must be presented on arrival. Near the hotel, Lupa's offers what are probably the best pizzas on the coast.

A large roundabout bridges the *carretera* immediately north of the casino, providing convenient access to San Agustín's market

SAN AGUSTIN

(*mercado*) and much of the town's accommodation. The next bridge across the highway in the direction of Playa del Inglés leads back to the coast and San Agustín's multi-storey shopping centre.

Five virtually identical bridges cross the *carretera* between Playa de Morro Besudo and Playa del Inglés; these can be confusing to strangers, and it is important that bus passengers staying in San Agustín soon learn to identify the bridge nearest the bus stop that they require. Fortunately, most will want either the third or the fourth bridge from the Playa del Inglés direction (the second or third from the Playa de Morro Besudo direction), and these are not be too difficult to identify as they are both located on a steep gradient.

One of the most attractive aspects of San Agustín is its beautifully maintained seafront promenade, which runs with very few breaks all the way to the sand dunes of Maspalomas. Much of the walk is verdant, as seafront buildings have been restricted to single storey level, ie bungalows, and their cacti and flower-bedecked walls and gardens are a delight.

A slender jetty signifies the beginning of the long **Playa de las Burras**, which merges imperceptibly, via El Cochino beach, with Playa del Inglés and the distant sand dunes. Parts of it, however, are dangerous for swimmers, who are better advised to make for the beaches further south. As the sun begins to sink, a virtual flotilla of fishing boats returns with the afternoon catch; this will not be sold to the public until very early the next morning, or part of it may often be seen drying in the sun.

Playa del Inglés

A wedge-shaped town, all of which lies to the south of the *carretera*, Playa del Inglés, it must be admitted, is not to everyone's taste. Basically, it should be regarded as a convenient dormitory that does not really come to life until sundown, when the bars, restaurants and shopping centres get into their swing — and stay swinging until the small hours. The winding street pattern of the town suggests a medieval foundation, but nothing could be further from the truth: Playa del Inglés is a modern conglomeration of individual, virtually uncontrolled developments, which have merged to form an architecturally repetitive, unplanned resort. It is a good thing, perhaps, that the town is so bereft of architectural appeal that few will wish to walk around it for pleasure, because to do so would present problems: there are few landmarks, and the streets end in cul de sacs, wind back on themselves and, worst of all, although road maps indicate that each one has a name, almost none is identified.

Playa del Inglés has no town centre, there are no parks, and few trees soften the utilitarian nature of the buildings, most of which are of concrete. At an early stage, it appears to have been decided that virtually all the shops had to be grouped together around sunken plazas in multi-storey developments, known as *Centro Commercials.* The result has been that the streets of the town present a monotonous repetition of 'international' bars, restaurants, hotels, fast-food outlets and postcard kiosks — but few shops. Tourist bungalow developments, of even greater monotony, make haphazard appearances without any apparent rhyme or reason.

It must be said that those who have booked, or are considering booking, a holiday based on Playa del Inglés, should not be too depressed by this unflattering description of the town's appearance. The great saviour of Playa del Inglés is its excellent bus services, which not only link all the shopping centres, but also provide easy access to other parts of the island. There is also a varied nightlife, excellent restaurants to suit all tastes and pockets and, of course, there is the superb all-year-round climate, the swimming pools, and the great sweep of golden sand, which merges with the picturesque dunes of Maspalomas.

The beach was formerly known as El Inglés (the Englishman)

due, it is said, to an eccentric Englishman who, some years ago, camped on it for many months in splendid isolation. A more prosaic explanation for the name is that English sailors landed there during the Napoleonic wars. It is certain, however, that 'Inglés' does not refer to English tourists, who are greatly outnumbered, particularly in the more expensive high season (winter), by Germans. In the summer, which is the cheaper, low season, the British, plus Spaniards escaping from their blisteringly hot mainland peninsula, are more numerous. It seems likely that the difference in wealth between the British and the Germans, rather than taste, is the main reason for this. Scandinavians, bent on escaping their dark, freezing winters, naturally prefer to visit the Canaries from December to May, and are spread fairly evenly among the south coast resorts.

Playa del Inglés has a high ratio of hotels to self-catering units, but surprisingly, only two of them, both four-star, directly overlook the beach: the Dunamar and the Riu Palace, the first of which has the unique advantage of a lift that transports guests the six floors between beach and street levels, thus avoiding the rather arduous climb that others (without cars) must make. Just in front of the Dunamar stretches the **Paseo Maritimo**, a half- ✳ mile stretch of bars and restaurants directly fronting the sea. There is also the occasional *supermercardo*, with high prices, which should only be patronised in emergencies.

The Riu Palace Hotel juts out at the most southerly tip of Playa del Inglés, and is the most convenient point from which to reach the sand dunes of Maspalomas, which it overlooks; there is a handy bus stop nearby. On the north side of the hotel, the main thoroughfare, Avenida de Tirajana, leads northward for almost two miles in a reasonably straight line, even crossing the *carretera* into the 'Spanish' suburb of San Fernando. Do not attempt to walk the rather uninteresting and tiring avenue from end to end in one go; buses traverse most of its length (although all except the 72 turn off westward at Plaza Telde, the avenue's last roundabout before the *carretera* is reached.

The centrally-located **Yumbo Centrum**, the largest shopping ✳ centre in Playa del Inglés, provides the town's most obvious landmark. *Yumbo* means enormous in Spanish, but apparently the word has lost, or never had, any connection with Jumbo, the

*above: Repairing fishing nets at El Cochino beach,
between San Agustín and Playa del Inglés*

opposite: San Agustín

famous elephant that gave its name to jumbo-sized in the English language. Visitors are confronted at the centre's main entrance (on the east side), therefore, not with the figure of an elephant but of a smiling dinosaur.

Visitors to the south of Gran Canaria are recommended to visit the Tourist Information Centre, situated on the south-east corner of the Yumbo Centrum, where the helpful staff can provide information about accommodation, public transport, car hire, restaurants, coach tours and special events.

After the shops close at around 9pm, the Yumbo Centrum's restaurants take over and the bars open, many of the latter being sparsely attended before midnight. The appearance of leather-clad men with bristling moustaches and shaven heads indicates the concentrated presence along the north stretch, at all levels, of almost all the south coast's gay bars — plus some primarily straight bars, which nevertheless specialize in drag acts. Although a handful of the gay bars are English-owned, the majority of patrons appear to be German.

As may be expected, many of the other establishments cater especially for the compatriots of their owners, particularly where they are Scandinavian; if food is provided, visitors will have the opportunity of sampling unfamiliar dishes at much lower prices than they would have to pay in Norway or Denmark, for example. Needless to say, there is little in the way of Canary, or even Spanish, food available.

Although Playa del Inglés has no real centre, at night the paved area facing the **Ecumenical Church of San Salvador** does provide an assembly point of sorts. The curved, aircraft-hangar form of the church provides the only architectural relief from straight lines to be seen in the town. Discos and shops abound in the **Kasbah** and **Metro** centres, which lie beside the church, and a lively atmosphere prevails.

This quarter is haunted by a multitude of young hustlers, who remorselessly try to inveigle acquiescent couples into viewing time-share properties with offers of free champagne, free lunches and similar incentives. Other presumptuous teenagers thrust leaflets promoting unremarkable bars, clubs and restaurants into your hands — do not get involved in discussing their merits as all are practically identical. It is better to work up a few

Shopping Centres in Playa del Inglés

The **Yumbo Centrum** is the largest shopping complex in Playa del Inglés, and is the town's most obvious landmark. The west side of the centre lies slightly back from Avenida de Tirajana, although the approach paths from it are poorly indicated and easily missed. The multi-storey complex is approximately rectangular, its north and south sides being almost twice the length of the other two.

Like most of the coastal shopping centres, the Yumbo Centrum combines supermarkets, boutiques and electronic/camera/watch shops, with bars and restaurants, most of which, but not all, are fast food establishments. Highly recommended for its reliability of quality and service throughout the island is **Vasari**, a duty-free shop where prices are fixed, guarantees are always given, and the genuine article, not an imitation, is assured. However, this is not to say that lower prices for the same item cannot be found elsewhere — by negotiation — but *caveat emptor*. Further advice regarding purchases is given in the Fact File.

Other shopping centres, although smaller, are similar in content and atmosphere. To the south of Yumbo Centrum lies **Cita**, to the south-east **Sandia** and to the east, facing each other, **Kasbah** and **Metro**. Metro is also known as Plaza de Maspalomas, after its central square, which is confusing as the centre is nowhere near Faro de Maspalomas. Among those who appear to have been confused are the Tourist Office: their plan not only indicates the wrong position of Plaza de Maspalomas, but also describes it as Maspalomas Town Square and Shopping Centre! At the eastern end of Playa del Inglés, just south of the *carretera*, are two more shopping centres, which adjoin: **El Viril** and **El Aguila**.

The four-star Dunamar is one of only two hotels in Playa del Inglés that directly overlook the beach

opposite: A colourful promenade, the Paseo Costa Canaria, runs from San Agustín to Playa del Inglés

Souvenir stalls line the Paseo Maritimo at Playa del Inglés

dismissive jokes, or give a polite thank you, rather than be offensive.

At Playa del Inglés, the coastal promenade is officially named **Paseo Costa Canaria** and this leads to the southern tip of the town, where the Riu Palace Hotel overlooks the famous sand dunes. It is much quicker to approach the dunes via this promenade than to follow the crocodile of holidaymakers that march towards them along the shoreline, bravely splashing their feet from time to time in the icy water.

Nowadays, the sand dunes begin at the point of the triangle that marks the southerly extent of the built-up area of Playa del Inglés, but they once extended further inland, until removed by the developers. Photographs of Las Palmas show that similar sand dunes existed at the northern end of the island until the 1950s, however, no trace of them remains. Until quite recently, it was believed that winds had lifted the Maspalomas sands from the Sahara desert and deposited them in their present position; however, a minute inspection of granules from both locations has revealed that their structures are dissimilar, and it now appears that the sands of Maspalomas are indigenous to Gran Canaria.

A spiky, leafless bush, resembling a ladies hairnet stretched out to dry, cacti and the occasional palm tree make up the 'flora' to be found at the northern end of the sand dunes. At this point, in spite of being much less heavily dressed than before, the same moustachiod, shaven-headed men (or their close relatives), who gather at night on the north side of the Yumbo Centrum, will be observed in great numbers. They are apparently botanical enthusiasts, and it is fascinating to watch them diving enthusiastically into the scrub in search of rare specimens!

Those who have strayed thus far from the shore should look out for the venomous 'crowns of thorns' hiding in the sand, which encloses the seeds of the spiky bushes found here. The object of the thorns is to attach themselves to passing animals with leathery skin; they do not feel a thing, but will later deposit the seeds at an uncompetive distance from the mother plant. But these needle-sharp thorns cause great agony to those humans who inadvertently step on them, so ensure that beach shoes are worn in this region.

Holidaymakers chosing Playa del Inglés as their base will probably find that, apart from price, four major factors will determine their selection of accommodation: proximity to the beach, proximity to the sand dunes, proximity to the night life, and the availability of a heated swimming pool. Virtually no one will be far from a bus route: the stop at Plaza de Maspalomas (opposite the Joya nightclub entrance) is the closest to the beach, and the stop at Plaza Fuerteventura (in front of the Riu Palace Hotel) is the closest to the sand dunes.

Night life is a different matter, as all bus services in the area, except the infrequent Las Palmas-Maspalomas 05 night bus, terminate shortly after 9pm. A central position, within easy walking distance of the Yumbo Centrum would probably be ideal for nightbirds. Taxis, of course, operate all night, but repeated use of them in the early hours of the morning, even for quite short distances, can eat into the holiday pesetas.

San Fernando

Although technically part of Maspalomas, this quarter, laid out to accommodate Canarios working in the resorts, has such a completely different atmosphere that it is better treated as a separate entity. Most will appproach it from Cruz de San Fernando, the large roundabout straddling the *carretera* at the north end of Avenida de Tirajana; the 72 bus links the quarter with most of Playa del Inglés (but not in the evening), and the more direct 03 and 31 buses, which follow the *carretera*, by-passing most of Playa del Inglés, are even more convenient for some.

Monstrously ugly blocks of apartments and offices are all that can be seen from the south side of the *carretera*, giving the impression that San Fernando has made desperate attempts to dissuade tourists from visiting it. Ignore these, for behind lies an extremely attractive housing estate, by far the most enjoyable *Centro Commercial* in the south, and a *Supermercardo* which is geared to local, rather than north European, tastes and incomes. There are also genuine *tapas* bars — or at least as genuine as the rather limited shellfish found in Canary waters permits, and several restaurants offer traditional Canary dishes. It is well worth crossing the *carretera* to visit the 'real Spain'.

*Sun worship at
Playa del Inglés*

*All-year-round is
outdoor café time at
Playa del Inglés*

A great number of restaurants line the Paseo Maritimo at Playa del Inglés

Overlooking the Cruz de San Fernando roundabout, Viude de Franco is an old-established Canary restaurant, which transferred to its present site from smaller but more picturesque premises some years ago; surprisingly, the original buildings still remain on the west side of the roundabout, surrounded by an unkempt garden. La Viude (the widow) apparently founded the establishment soon after her husband, Franco, had died. It would seem that the Spanish dictator took no exception to the implication that he himself might have passed away, as he personally initiated San Fernando's local authority housing development immediately behind the restaurant. Its streets, although uniform and set to a grid pattern, are most appealing, and their sub-tropical gardens a delight.

Refreshingly intimate in scale without being too small, the shopping centre of San Fernando appeals mainly because it is, in essence, a village high street, which actually incorporates shops selling goods that people living there need. Differences between this centre and the entirely tourist-inspired versions along the coast are really quite subtle, but the overall ambience is incomparably more natural, human — and Spanish. At the rear of the centre is La Bodeguita del Medio — probably the best *tapas* bar in the south, and an excellent spot for lunch — go easy on the drinks, however, which are very much cheaper than in tourist land.

On arrival in the south, an early visit to San Fernando's Ansoco supermarket is strongly recommended. Load up with as much as possible, and invest in a taxi for the return journey. Even those who are not self-catering will find that the prices of alcohol, soft drinks, biscuits and confectionery are much lower here than at most other places in the south, and there is also a wide range of Spanish charcuterie and cheeses available for lunchtime sandwiches.

Several restaurants, most of them offering local Canary specialities, stretch eastward along the *carretera* from La Viude de Franco, Chó Pedro probably being one of the most authentic. However, Pepe el Breca, on the main road to Fataga, is generally regarded as the best (and most expensive) of San Fernando's restaurants.

Technically in San Fernando, but in essence straying from

Playa del Inglés, are two much more tourist orientated commercial centres overlooking the *carretera*, **Nilo** and **Euro Centers**. In the latter, at number 20-22, two-seater 'trikes' may be hired from Rent a Trike — a driving licence and passport are needed

Maspalomas

Simply meaning 'more pigeons', Maspalomas refers to the migrating birds — not only pigeons — that take a break on the lagoon of the Maspalomas oasis before continuing their journey from Europe to their winter quarters. In recent years, boating holidaymakers have somewhat reduced their numbers. Officially, Maspalomas covers the region immediately west of Playa del Inglés, but to most the name denotes only the area around the *faro* (lighthouse), the lagoon and the sand dunes.

Until the mid 1950s, Maspalomas was a centre for tomato growing: the ever-present sunshine and absence of frosts ensured all-year-round crops. Tourism, however, proved to be more profitable, and three luxury-grade hotels now stand where tomatoes formerly ripened. One of these hotels, the Maspalomas Oasis, has retained its five-star rating for many years; only two other hotels on the coast have a similar high grade: the Meliá Tamarindos at San Agustín and the La Canaria, outside Puerto Rico. No other hotels have been permitted in the Faro de Maspalomas area, which therefore has remained very exclusive. During the day, however, masses of holidaymakers, supplemented on Sundays by Las Palmas sunworshippers, trek from the bus terminal at Plaza del Faro to the beach. The *paseo* is lined with souvenir shops and restaurants — prices are surprisingly reasonable.

On their first visit, most make for the ancient lighthouse, ✳ which remains the south coast's one important landmark. It is not apparent where the beach of Maspalomas joins that of Playa del Inglés, almost the entire stretch being lined with virtually identical sunbeds and parasols, which double as useful windbreaks. On the east side of the lighthouse is the still picturesque oasis of **Charca de Maspalomas**, the edges of its lagoon fringed with feathery pampas grass. Behind this rise the first of the sand dunes. The walk across them to the southern tip of Playa del

Island of contrasts: the great sand beach at Maspalomas, with its dunes and dramatic mountainous background

Ever on the move, the sand dunes of Maspalomas are at their most sinuous in the late evening sunshine

The pampas grass fringed freshwater lagoon at Maspalomas is only a stone's throw from the teeming beaches

Inglés may not appear to be long, but at least an hour should be allowed, as the sands cling tiringly to the feet, even if the larger dunes are avoided.

Many find the dunes to be at their most impressive early in the morning, when the tourists' footprints of the previous day have been filled in by the drifting sand, and the low sun casts sensuous, undulating shadows. As may be expected, camel rides provide a popular 'mini Sahara' trip among the dunes, and make good souvenir photographs. There is even a camel safari from the Maspalomas sand dunes into the mountains, as far as Arteara and Fataga.

Nude sunbathing is officially permitted in the dunes away from the beach and also in a designated section of **Playa de la Mujer**, west of the lighthouse, where most of the nudists are German. Many Germans have an ingrained belief that to give an airing to parts of the body that do not normally get one is a good and healthy thing to do. It is fairly apparent, from what is on view, that vanity can have little part to play in their enthusiasm; those who have ever suffered traumas after accidentally surprising grandma in the bath might be advised to give both the dunes and the designated areas a wide berth!

Westward from the lighthouse, the beach becomes dangerous, due to the occasional whirlpools that form a short distance out to sea — swimmers should avoid the area.

Additional Information

Accommodation
Don Miguel Hotel ***
30 Avenida Tirajana
Playa del Inglés
☎ 761508

Ifa Dunamar Hotel ****
8 Helsinki
Playa del Inglés
☎ 761200

*Iberotel Maspalomas Oasis
    Hotel* *****
Playa de Maspalomas
☎ 141448

Meliá Tamarindos Hotel *****
3 Retama
San Agustín
☎ 762600

Eating out
Chó Pedro
Marcial Franco 12
San Fernando
☎ 77 02 68
Open: daily 14pm and 5-12pm

Bali
Av de Tarajana
Playa del Inglés
☎ 76 32 61
Open: daily 5-11pm
Indonesian cuisine.

Casa Gallega
Marcial Franco 12
Playa del Inglés
☎ 76 20 92
Open: 1-4pm, 7pm-midnight
Galician Spanish cuisine.

Things to Do
Fataga Camel Safari
Barranco de Arteara 5-7
Fataga
☎ 79 86 86 / 79 86 98

Tourist Information Office
Yumbo Centrum
Playa del Inglés
☎ 76 78 48
Open: Monday-Saturday 9am-3pm

The South-West Coast Resorts

2

Las Meloneras

Soon after the Faro de Maspalomas, a path stretches westward above the cliffs in the direction of Playa de las Meloneras. Below lie strangely-shaped rocks, which are much favoured by sunbathers. Gradually, the path veers northward and, after a 25-minute walk, a descent can be made to the small beach of Las Meloneras. Protection from east and north winds is given by the surrounding hills, and there is a popular beachfront restaurant, Casa Serafin, from where sunbeds and parasols may be hired. Nudism is permitted at the south end of the bay.

above: The marina at Puerto de Mogán

opposite: Pasito Blanco, a resort designed for the yachting fraternity

Pasito Blanco

The main coastal road continues westward; those with private vehicles in search of very secluded sunbathing can turn left and follow an unpaved track to a 500m long beach of fine, clean sand at **El Hornillo**.

Pasito Blanco's marina, also reached by a side road, gives added protection to the small cove in which its beach is set, and the water is therefore calmer and clearer than usual around this coast: it is, in consequence, popular with scuba divers. An extensive camping park behind the marina, rare in the Canaries, provides virtually all the local accommodation.

Arguineguin

The main road soon skirts the coast, and ahead can be seen the cement works of Arguineguin, which completely disfigures Santa Agueda Bay. Fortunately, it is out of sight of most of Arguineguin itself. Many will be tempted to visit Arguineguin, as this is the only example of a genuine fishing village on the coast between San Agustín and Puerto de Mogán. However, apart from a promenade beween the harbour and the beach, it cannot be described as picturesque, and the beach is dreary. Nevertheless, Arguineguin's *tapas* bars are genuine enough and the port can be lively. As may be expected, the local restaurants are renowned for the freshness and quality of fish served, particularly *vieja*. A large, open-air market is held every Tuesday morning.

Patalavaca

Patavalaca developed behind a small jetty from which tomatoes were formerly shipped to Las Palmas, connections by road then being extremely tortuous. Now, the town almost entirely comprises hotels and apartment blocks, which are mainly patronized by Scandinavian holidaymakers. The coastal promenade between Arguineguin and Patalavaca is most pleasant. Patalavaca's chief attraction lies in its clean beach, the sand being unusually pale for the area.

Puerto Rico

It is only a short distance along the main road to Puerto Rico. On route is passed the La Canaria Hotel, a surprising location for a five-star establishment. The road enters a tunnel and then, at its end, a superb view of the favourite resort of the British in Gran Canaria is revealed. An even more dramatic approach can be made by sea, either from Arguineguin or Puerto de Mogán, but few make their initial contact with Puerto Rico in this way. Puerto Rico means rich port, which it certainly never was until the possibilities of its micro-climate — significantly more anual sunshine than Playa del Inglés — and its protection from most winds by embracing hills, suggested tourist development.

The first move was to create an outstandingly attractive beach, and tons of golden sand were shipped in from the Sahara Desert in tankers. A new road to Playa del Inglés and thence to the airport and Las Palmas was laid out, and the developers moved in. Unfortunately flat land was limited, and gradually, with no obvious restrictions imposed, white apartment blocks climbed up the hillsides. From the centre of the town, it is rather like being on stage in an Ancient Greek amphitheatre of gigantic proportions.

Apart from one delightful *apartotel*, all the accommodation in Puerto Rico is self-catering, tariffs in general falling with the altitude of the building occupied. Tour operators offer some amazingly cheap package tours to the resort from the UK in winter outside the Christmas/New Year period, but almost all of them perch their clients in the very highest located buildings — great views but an arduous approach. Buses wind up the steep hillsides at fairly regular intervals (although not at night). However, the fittest generally walk down (hoping that something vital — such as money — has not been forgotten) and travel back up by bus.

Buses connect Las Palmas and all the intervening coastal resorts with Puerto Rico, depositing visitors in the town centre; most then immediately make their way through the adjacent park to the beach. This is a unique and most praiseworthy feature of the town, incorporating children's play areas, tennis courts and many examples of Canarian flora. The mature trees

Arguineguin has a busy fishing harbour

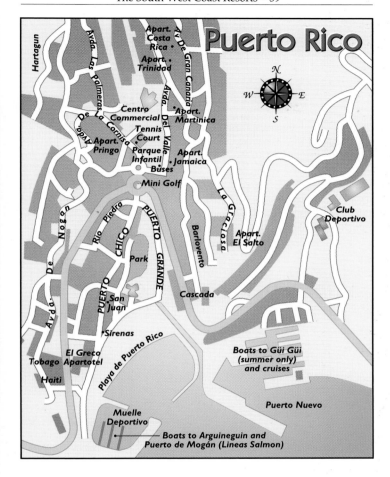

provide a welcoming splash of green, which is unmatched by the other south coast resorts.

With its concentration on low-cost self-catering apartments and a safe beach of golden sand, Puerto Rico is primarily aimed at the young family market, and far more children will be seen here than anywhere else in the Canaries. In consequence, the night life is extremely limited, and Puerto Rico is surely one of the very few towns in Spain where, by law, all bar and restaurants must set the volume of their music at a low level. As there is no late-night public transport to Playa del Inglés this resort is not suitable as a base for those youngsters who crave ear-splitting music from dawn to dawn.

Throughout most of the year, Puerto Rico's famous golden beach can only be seen in its entirety early and late in the day. In between, as long as the sun is shining, it is concealed by hundreds of minimally-clad, prostrate bodies, so closely packed together on their sunbeds that only with great skill can an international incident be avoided when attempting to zig-zag between them. From the little that can be glimpsed of it, a dispassionate observer might wonder if the great expense of transporting the sand all the way from Africa was really worthwhile!

The main **port** is approached from the north side of the beach, and it is from here that most game-fishing expeditions depart. All set sail early in the morning, returning with their catches mid-afternoon, to be greeted with much excitement. Also from here, boat trips are run at half-hourly intervals by Lineas Salmon to Puerto Mogán or Arguineguin (return fares only). It is well worth taking both trips on separate days, although the former is rather more spectacular — look out for enormous caves in the volcanic cliffs.

The town's second port, **Puerto Nuevo**, can be reached by walking across the attractive pedestrian bridge over the tidal stream, which borders the south side of the beach. From here, departing at 10.30am, a whole day cruise can be made on the red-sailed windjammer *San Miguel*, with lunch included. Motorized vessels also offer shark-fishing excursions further out to sea. In summer only, trips are made to Güi-Güi beach, the island's most secluded, where a barbecue lunch is provided (see page 73). Back in the town centre, just behind the park, is the **Centro Commercial** of Puerto Rico. The usual dismal concrete development accommodates the resort's shops and entertainment facilities. Here also are located the most ambitious of Puerto Rico's restaurants.

While those staying in Puerto Rico are unlikely to find its protected beach windswept, the sea water is no warmer than elsewhere. Due to the smaller units built and lower prices charged, much of the accommodation in Puerto Rico does not include a heated swimming pool, which virtually rules out bathing in the winter. The top spot to stay is the El Greco Apartotel, sited at beach level, which does have a large, heated pool, as well as maid service and restaurants.

As at Playa del Inglés time-share touts abound, but do not be fooled by your apparent sucess in winning a competition — everyone is a 'winner'.

The one compensation for the overdevelopment of apartments on Puerto Rico's enveloping hills can only be appreciated after sunset, when most day visitors have left. As the lights are turned on one by one, the hillsides twinkle in a magical way, evoking the early years of Hong Kong.

Puerto de Mogán

The 812 road from Puerto Rico to Puerto de Mogán winds close to the shore, providing occasional glimpses of small bays, some with tourist developments completed or underway; none, however, are of particular interest, and few will wish to visit them. Immediately north of Puerto Rico, overlooking **Playa de Tauro**, the camping site of Guantanamo, with a capacity of 150, is the largest on the island. Before the modern road was laid out, Puerto de Mogán's connection with other parts of the adjacent coast was by sea. Puerto de Mogán is quite small, and a large percentage of visitors are day trippers who are based elsewhere along the south coast. As has already been indicated, a return boat trip from either Puerto Rico or Arguineguin is the most impressive way to arrive at this delightful resort, with its dramatic background of the lush, steeply-rising Barranco de Mogán.

The first enthralling view of the marina is so unbelievable that the visitor experiences a sense of trauma, followed by puzzlement. After what has been seen elsewhere on the coast of Gran Canaria, what has led to the creation of a modern development that actually enhances it? Just about everything seems right: low-rise buildings, mostly serving as self-catering units, have been laid out along the banks of narrow canals, linked by

*With its golden beach and natural protection from most winds, sunny
Puerto Rico is a great favourite with British holidaymakers*

Puerto Rico's apartments cover the surrounding hillsides

Purto de Mogán's original port survives behind the modern marina; in the background stretches the fertile Mogán valley

Puerto de Mogán, designed in traditional style, is reminiscent of a Spanish fishing village on the Atlantic coast

Venetian-style bridges. The walls of the buildings have been smothered with flowers, and exotic plants grow in small garden plots; arches pretending to act as buttresses span the walkways. Most unusual of all, the flat surrounds to windows and doors have been painted bright colours, as if they were architraves. The effect of this is reminiscent of the small Atlantic fishing ports between Cádiz and the Portuguese frontier, where the relief fron the dead-white, undecorated houses that dominate southern Spain's Mediterranian coast is equally welcome.

Those arriving by road have a far less spectacular introduction, coming in by the back door so to speak. On the left is the beach, a not particularly appealing affair of grey sand, dredged up from the sea to provide, rather grudgingly it seems, somewhere for visitors to obtain their tans — sunbeds may be hired, but there are no adjacent bars or other facilities. The impression is given that the beach has been kept low-key deliberately, in order to dissuade mere sun worshippers from taking over the town, which was specifically planned for boating enthusiasts. Day-visitors are therefore recommended to make their trip to Puerto Mogán on a non-beach day, and appreciate the resort's alternative, unique attractions. Most will wander, initially, around the marina's canals, revelling in the shops, bars and restaurants, which are located in a refreshing, higgledy-piggledy way — Puerto de Mogán has no ghastly ghetto of a *Centro Commercial*.

The marina was built in front of an existing fishing port, on reclaimed land, and the original buildings were left untouched. Behind the waterfront restaurants it is pleasant to climb the narrow streets of old Puerto de Mogán which, although small, is the only village on the south coast to possess any real charm. Originally, the sea lapped the old port, but it was pushed back to accommodate the new road, waterside buildings and the esplanade in front of them.

Try to find the small Bar Manolo, approached up steps, which few holidaymakers seem to discover. Very spartan, it is run by Manolo and his son, who seem to operate a running feud, which can be quite alarming until it is appreciated that all is good-natured fun, punctuated at intervals by the exchange of smacking kisses on both cheeks. The prices are almost embarrassingly low, and at least one, simple hot dish is generally available. Although nothing but Spanish is understood, foreigners are given a friendly welcome — the real Canaries at last!

Let us return now to the green, blue and ochre painted surrounds of the windows and doors already observed on the new buildings of the marina. It will be noted that some of the houses of the former port have the same feature, which certainly appears nowhere else along the coast. One wonders if this Moorish style of decoration is original to the old town and inspired its adoption by the architect of the marina, or whether the reverse occurred, residents of the original buildings, attracted by what they saw, deciding to brighten up the façades of their own houses in a similar way.

Sol Club de Mar operates the holidaymaker's apartments on the marina as well as the superbly located hotel to the south of it, from which there are exquisite views across the bay towards the headland. The hotel's swimming pool complex, which is most elegant, may also be used by those staying in the apartments, as may also the hotels's other facilities, which include an excellent restaurant. As Puerto Mogán's sunshine record is similar to that of Puerto Rico — some say even better — those seeking a relaxing holiday amidst idyllic surroundings, without insisting on a golden beach or swinging discos, will find Puerto de Mogán hard to match anywhere in the Canary Islands.

Lineas Salmon's boat trips along the coast pick up and deposit passengers at the southerly point of the harbour but, on the opposite jetty, near the lighthouse, is docked the Yellow Submarine, a vessel manufactured in Finland in 1988 specifically for viewing marine life. Apprehensive voyagers are lulled by soft music as the boat sinks slowly below sea level. An instant 'coral reef' has been created by sinking a wreck, which is popular as a hideaway for smaller fish as it provides a refuge from large predators. The trip lasts approximately 45 minutes — the cost of tickets, however, is not inconsiderable. For those booking a trip on the Yellow Submarine in advance there is a free bus service from Puerto Rico and the major hotels in Playa del Inglés.

Additional Information

Accommodation

El Greco Apartotel AT (two keys)
Puerto Chico
Puerto Rico
☎ 749214

Sol Club de Mar Hotel***
Puerto de Mogán
☎ 56 50 66

Eating out

Oliver
Shopping Centre
Puerto Rico
☎ 74 53 45
Open: 6.30-10.30pm (not Tuesdays)

Tu Casa
Puerto de Mogán
☎ 74 00 74
Open: 12 noon-12 midnight (not Tuesdays)

Boat Trips

Lineas Salmon
Leaves Puerto Rico daily at 11am, 12 noon, 1, 2, 3, 4pm for Puerto de Mogán; returns at 11.45am, 12.45, 1.45, 2.45, 3.45, 4.45pm.
Leaves Puerto Rico daily at 10.30am, 12.30, 2.30, 4.30pm for Arguineguin; returns at 11.15am, 1.15, 3.15, 5pm.
Check times locally.

Yellow Submarine
Puerto de Mogán
☎ 56 51 08 / 56 50 48 for reservation and free bus.

Itineraries In The South

3

The following itineraries, all begining and ending at the south coast resorts, have been selected bearing in mind that the majority of holidaymakers may not have the use of a motor vehicle. Unless specifically mentioned, therefore, all locations may be reached via buses operated by the Salcai line. Towards the north of the island, most Salcai buses interconnect with those operated by Utinsa, the routes of which begin and end at Las Palmas. Resorts along the south coast have been described in a clockwise direction ending at Puerto de Mogán; all the following excursions, however, which can be made from any of them, will be described in anti-clockwise order from Puerto de Mogán and ending north of San Agustín. Holidaymakers based at Las Palmas will find it easier and quicker to explore the central mountain range from there rather than from the south.

Due to the terrain, most hiking expeditions in Gran Canaria tend to become rather strenuous affairs once the roads have been left. For enthusiastic walkers, a great deal of advice regarding clothing and detailed topographical features is essential. Such advice, outside the scope of this book, is given in *Landscapes of Gran Canaria* by Noel Rochford, published by Sunflower Books.

The Western Barrancos & Coast

Mogán• Pie de la Cuesta • San Nicolás de Tolentino (or Aldea San Nicolás) • Puerto de la Aldea

The 810 road from Puerto de Mogán connects the locations on this itinerary, and is followed by the 38 bus from Las Palmas, which may be joined at San Agustín or San Fernando, but not at Playa del Inglés, as it keeps to the *carretera*. Buses 84 and 86 link Puerto de Mogán with Mogán, as does bus 01 or 02, which begins at Arguineguin and may be joined at Puerto Rico.

Puerto de Mogán came into existence as the port from which the agricultural produce of the fertile Mogán valley behind it was shipped to the other ports of the island; it was not, primarily, a fishing port. Until tourism led to the recent construction of the coast road, the south-west of Gran Canaria was extremely isolated.

Mogán & its Valley

The elevated village of Mogán, after which the now much larger port is named, has inevitably been affected by tourism, and establishments offering souvenirs and the usual 'international' dishes have proliferated. However, Mogán is still attractive and certainly worth a halt.

The 810 from Puerto de Mogán follows the Mogán valley, which is one of the most fertile and beautiful in Gran Canaria. Here will be found aubergines, papayas, avocados, mangoes and coffee in abundance. It seems strange that the almost rainless port should be located so near to this well-watered region, but clouds will often begin to appear as the mountain peaks rising behind Mogán are approached, and heavy showers

previous page: Roque Bentaiga near Tejeda

regularly develop, particularly on winter afternoons, filling the ducted streams which irrigate the valley.

The green upper reaches of the ravine are so idyllic that, on their return journey to the coast, many bus passengers are tempted to follow it by alighting at Mogán and walking down-hill to Puerto de Mogán (9km, 6 miles). Unfortunately, there are no public footpaths, the land on either side of the road being divided into numerous smallholdings, many of which are defended by barking dogs. Although none of them will be rabid, their apparent ferocity can be alarming, and there have been occasional reports of intrepid tourists being bitten. It is better to view the exotic crops from the road, or the terrace of the Acaymo restaurant, which overlooks the ravine to the south of Mogán and is considered one of the best in the region. The main road, therefore, must be kept to by those following the valley on foot, and as this is used by a constant stream of vehicles, the experience is hardly worth the effort — even though the occasional brief escape into dogless plantations on either side can be made. It is an unfortunate fact that practically all of Gran Canaria's fertile ravines similarly lack footpaths leading to the coast.

Pie de la Cuesta

This hamlet stands at the head of the Mogán valley, its small restaurant, El Aurillo, retaining a Canarian ambience. For those with (preferably four-wheel-drive) vehicles, and strong nerves, the extremely narrow 811, right, leads north-eastward. The lower reaches of the road have been recently surfaced, but as the road zig-zags steeply it develops into an unsurfaced track with precipitous drops, despite being shown as a good road on some maps. It passes between two reservoirs with spectacular views, before improving and eventually meeting up with the 815, which penetrates the dramatic central heights of the island (see page 84). This scenic area is best approached from the north.

Veneguera & its Valley

Most, however, will opt to proceed westward in the direction of San Nicolás after leaving Pie de la Cuesta. The Barranco de Veneguera soon stretches towards the coast, and a side road, the 10.2, branches off to Veneguera village, a small cluster of

The Mogán valley, where many of the island's exotic crops are grown

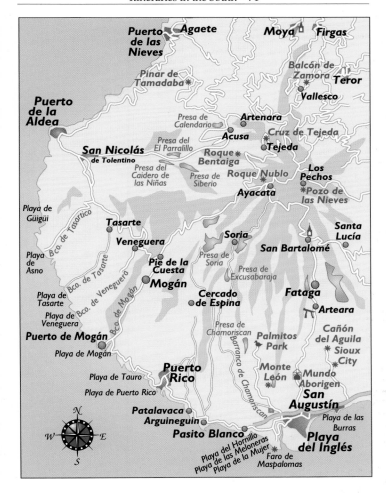

Moorish-style white houses at the *barranco*'s head. Unfortunately, this road soon becomes little more than a track — do not believe the wildly over-optimistic maps — and a four-wheel-drive vehicle is needed to follow the *barranco* to Playa de

Veneguera in comfort. The remote valley of Veneguera is remarkable for the abundance of candelabra cacti (*cardón*), evocative of an American Wild West film.

 Not only geologists will be impressed by the famous multicoloured strata of the mountainsides, which betray their volcanic origins; they can be seen from the 810 between the villages of Veneguera and Tasarte. Predominant colours are pastel green and pink, but other hues also make an appearance; nowhere else in the Canaries is such mineral exuberance displayed.

Two more valleys now swing away westward towards the coast; they are named after their respective villages, Tasarte and Tasartico. (See the next section.)

San Nicolás de Tolentino & Puerto de la Aldea

After the Tasartico branch road has been passed, the 810 descends to the market town of San Nicolás de Tolentino, lying in the wide valley of the Barranco de la Aldea. There is not a great deal to see in this small town, even though passing tourists are catered for. As in much of southern Spain, extensive plastic sheeting has been stretched over the tomatoes, which increases the yield, but at the expense of gravely disfiguring the environment; few will wish to trek through this plastic landscape. The town is alternatively referred to as Aldea de San Nicolás.

As San Nicolás has little to detain visitors for long, most will soon continue the short distance to Puerto de la Aldea, a peaceful fishing harbour, with a small, dark-sand beach protected by cliffs. Look out for its Peñon Bermejo, a vase-shaped rock. It was at Puerto de la Aldea that the fossilized remains of the Verdino dog, over 2,000 years old, were discovered.

Every September, the local community converges on Puerto de la Aldea to take part in the Fiesta del Charco, casting palm leaves into the sea to ensure good crops the following year.

Bus 115 runs between San Nicolás and Puerto de la Aldea (but not very frequently) and the Utinsa bus 101, which ends its north coast journey from Las Palmas at San Nicolás, goes most of the way to it, but keeps to the 810; it is also a very restricted service. Taxis can easily be hired at San Nicolás, although only with some difficulty at Puerto de la Aldea.

Those without their own transport who wish to proceed further along the north coast are recommended not to be too ambitious in one day. No further than Puerto de las Nieves, plus perhaps the adjacent town of Agaete, should be attempted if returning southward by the 38 bus. It is, of course, possible to return to the south coast via Las Palmas if preferred — a much longer journey in distance although not in time, particularly if a south-east rather than a south-west coast resort is the final destination. Details of the northward continuation from San Nicolás are given (from Las Palmas) on pages 136-145.

The West Coast Beaches

Tasarte Beach & Asno Beaches

From Puerto de Mogán there is no coastal road northward until Puerto de la Aldea is reached. However, as already noted, narrow side roads, the 16.3 and the 16.5 respectively, branch off the 810, and follow the *barrancos* of Tasarte and Tasartico, providing motor access to the small, secluded beaches of Tasarte and Asno, both of which comprise grey sand with some gravel. Bus 86 from Puerto de Mogán follows the 810 in the direction of San Nicolás, and then branches left at Tasarte, continuing to its beach. Even smaller and more secluded beaches exist, but these can only be reached by experienced hikers or by boat.

Güi Güi Beach

At the time of writing, there is a tourist boat that departs, in summer only, from Puerto de Mogan to Güi Güi, considered to be the most appealing of all the beaches on this part of the coast. Güi Güi is overlooked by jagged peaks, and there are absolutely no facilities; organisers of the trip therefore provide a picnic lunch, which is included in the excursion price. The coastline passed is most dramatic, consisting of mountain ridges punctuated by ravines — and nothing else — no ports and, once Playa de Veneguera has been passed, little sign of any human presence. It is virgin Canary coastline, unmatched elsewhere on the island. A word of warning to poor sailors — the seas can be rough, which is why there are no trips in winter.

Cercado de Espino & Presa de Soria

The occasional bus 01 or 02 from Arguineguin follows the 12.3 road into the mountains as far as the village of Cercado de Espino, but a lengthy hike or four-wheel-drive vehicle is necessary to continue on the 10.3 to the Presa de Soria reservoir.

*Palmitos Park boasts
exotic birds, orchids,
butterflies and an
extensive cacti garden*

*opposite: Ayaguares
and its reservoirs can
be reached on foot from
Palmitos Park*

Beginning with the familiar aridity of the south, the Barranco de Arguineguin soon becomes fertile, greenery almost reaching the mountain tops. The usual Canary crops are grown in the valley, supplemented — as the hamlet of **El Sao** is reached — by vines. The village of **Cercado de Espino**, perched in the mountains, lies just off the road. Surprisingly, in view of its remoteness, the village's restaurant, Castillo Ramón, attracts daily tourist excursions between 12.30pm and 4pm, and is better given a miss during this period. Friday and Saturday nights become even more commercial, with folk dancing and singing. Although pine trees (*pino*) are certainly in evidence, it is the lofty palm trees which claim attention.

Those without a suitable vehicle will find the long walk from the village to **Presa de Soria** rather arduous, and it should not be attempted by the unfit; however, the reservoir's isolation will attract many. **Soria** is a tiny village (with a *tapas* bar) from which a short pathway leads to its reservoir. The return journey to Cercado de Espino on foot will be less tiring, as it is mostly downhill. Bus return times to Arguineigin should be confirmed with the driver in advance.

Palmitos Park, Ocean Park, Gran Karting

A visit to Palmitos Park, with the possible exception of a trip to Las Palmas, is the most popular of all the excursions from the southern resorts — and understandably so. Bus 45 runs from Playa del Inglés to the park, its route occasionally being diverted to Faro de Maspalomas (but with the same number, so be sure that the return destination is the one required). The bus stops served bear the legend 'Palmitos Park Bus', but other buses also use the stop: there is now no non-stop or limited stop service to Palmitos Park. From Puerto Rico, the 72 bus provides a direct service.

Ocean Park

On route is Ocean Park, a water park aimed at families with young children: the usual water tobogans and splashing spectaculars are a delight to youngsters (who are admitted at half price).

Gran Karting

At Gran Karting, a short distance away, mini tracks and mini vehicles have been designed so that even the under-fives can participate in go-carting with complete safety. For those over ten years old, specially designed mini motorbikes, claimed to be the first in Europe, provide a unique thrill.

Palmitos Park

This 200,000 sq m park, predominantly an aviary, is set at the head of the steep Barranco de Chamoriscan; a reservoir is located not far to the west, and springs and pools abound within the reservation. There are now estimated to be around 1,500 exotic birds from all parts of the world on view in the park, one-third of them flying freely; 230 different species are represented. Outstandingly popular are the flamingoes, toucans, crested cranes and the Inca cockatoos. Try not to miss the free 25-minute show (eight per day) given by macaws, which have been trained to perform extraordinary tricks.

Almost as impressive as the birds is the sub-tropical vegetation, equally international in nature, which includes towering cacti and fifty-one types of palm tree. A recent addition to Palmitos Park is the Tropical Butterfly House, Europe's largest, where hundreds of butterflies and moths fly freely.

From Palmitos Park a hike may be made into the next valley to the east by taking the road past the sports hotel overlooking the park. Follow the track round to the right and down to the village of **Ayaguares** near the dam of the lower of two reservoirs, returning the same way back to Palmitos Park.

During the return journey to the coast, high up on the left may be glimpsed the **Monte León** estate, Gran Canaria's most exclusive residential development (so exclusive that no maps refer to it); all the properties are set within extensive, sub-tropical grounds. For some reason, Monte León became extremely popular with eminent classical musicians, and a small, privately-run concert hall has been incorporated. A regular winter resident here was the late Leonard Bernstein.

Towards the High Mountains

Mundo Aborigen (Guanche Museum) • *Arteara* • *Fataga*
• *San Bartolomé de Tirajana*

This excursion follows the Carretera de Fataga (road 12.1), a continuation of Avenida de Tirajana. From Playa del Inglés, bus 48 makes the 6 kilometre journey to Mundo Aborigen.

Mundo Aborigen

Mundo Aborigen (Native World), of which the Canarios are very proud, is an open-air museum depicting the life of the island's original inhabitants, the Guanches. It is tempting to speculate that this venture may have been an attempt to counter-act the almost complete absence of cultural features along the south coast. Whatever the reason, the museum, spread over a hillside, primarily consists of wax or wooden models of Guanches doing useful things. Opened in 1994, it is now an established attraction for those with an interest in the archipela-go's history, and particularly local children on school outings.

Included in the admission fee is an extremely well-presented booklet in English, which describes each of the twenty-eight sectors as they are passed: visitors are sensibly recommended to follow a sequential route. Although of interest, the brief guide to Canary flora and birdlife included in the booklet is unfortu-nately not illustrated.

A summary of what is known (in some cases surmised) about the history of the Guanches has been given the Introduction, and it is the aim of the museum to bring to life aspects of their daily existence, including that of the regional leaders (*faycans*) and members of the royal family (*guanarteme*).

As may be expected, many of the exhibits relate to agriculture and husbandry, and an enormous black pig (alive, not a wax model), believed to be of the type reared by the Guanches, will stick in the minds of younger visitors in particular.

The religion of the Guanches seems to have been basically monotheistic, the Creator receiving a little help from the cosmic

opposite: Wax models at Mundo Aborigen open-air museum depict the daily life of the Guanches — the original inhabitants of Gran Canaria

elements in running the world. It was believed that death was merely a coma from which the body would eventually awake. Mummification and safe burial in caves and rock tombs was therefore regarded as supremely important, so that the bodies of the deceased when brought back to life would not have too many parts missing or badly damaged.

Carpentry, pottery, stoneworking, tanning and fibre processing were highly developed, but the Guanches remained completely ignorant of metalwork. Due to an innate fear of the sea, the Guanches were not navigators, deep-sea fishing and even journeys between the islands apparently being beyond them.

The gargantuan pig is not the only real-life exhibit in the complex. A Canario demonstrates for much of the day how the Guanches used poles to help them leap, kangaroo-like, through the difficult terrain. His costume looks as if his evening job is playing the lead in a touring production of Robinson Crusoe!

Within a few months of the museum's opening, information panels mounted within display boards began to fade to an untintelligible degree — it is hoped that this problem will be overcome.

The 48 bus terminates at Mundo Aborigen, but the 18 bus, which starts at San Fernando — outside the pharmacy in Avenida de Tirajana just after this has emerged from the north side of the Carretera del Sur — continues northward to Fataga, San Bartolomé de Tirajana and Ayacata. At the time of writing, however, in order to make a useful connection, the first 48 bus, leaving Playa del Inglés for Mundo Aborigen at 9.30am, will have to have been taken, thus limiting viewing time in the complex to around two hours.

Arteara

The Barranco de Fataga, climbing ever upward from San Fernando to San Bartolomé de Tirajana is, for much of its length, one of the most dramatic and vertiginous in Gran Canaria. Some find the short stretch as far as Mundo Aborigen exciting enough, but it is after this that the hairs on the back of the neck stand on end, the mouth goes dry, and one thinks fondly of the folks back home. Surely, no vehicle can negotiate that bend! How could any approaching car avoid head-on contact? The sheer drop must be over 1,000ft (300m) — and there are no protective walls! The shrill screams of tourists on the bus give great amusement to the locals, many of whom travel for much of the route at least twice a day without even bothering to glance out of the window. Sufferers from vertigo have been warned!

Some motorists, inspired by what they have learned about Guanche burials at Mundo Aborigen, may wish to halt at the easily-missed hamlet of **Arteara**, which lies in the valley shortly before Fataga is reached. Near the Arteara bus stop, a path tracks south-westward from the road, and the second right turn, which passes a solitary house, leads to a ruined Guanche necropolis, ⊓ many tons of disturbed stones contrasting dramatically with the verdant palm trees.

Surprisingly, archaelogists have not yet made their presence felt here, but one day, no doubt, areas will be roped-off for excavation, layouts and artists' impressions displayed and a more meaningful, but less virginal, site presented to the public. At the time of writing, however, it is primarily the sheer mass of stone that impresses.

Fataga

Sited on a low hill rising from the floor of the *barranco*, Fataga is a delight. Dark blocks of volcanic stone are revealed in the walls of the houses, thus enlivening the white plasterwork, a typical Canary feature. Most of the village lies on the west side of the main road, its cobbled streets winding around the occasional smallholding. Unlike Playa del Inglés, the name of even the shortest thoroughfare is proudly displayed. A large restaurant on the main road caters primarily for tourists, its prices and 'international' menus rivalling those along the coastal strip. Opposite this, however, is the village bar, its daily *tapas* menu chalked on a board. Often included are snails, goats meat in garlic, *papas arrugadas* and a home-made *mojo verde* sauce, but check out the food situation with the patron's wife, who does the cooking, as the friendly young barman is not always too sure exactly what his mum is up to in the kitchen. Bus passengers will arrive at Fataga around lunchtime, and many of them will wish to spend some time here before exploring the village (establish with certainty the return bus times).

In contrast to the fierce dogs guarding the valley's agricultural estates, Fataga's domestic animals have an exceptionally sweet nature. Strangers are greeted by dogs with tails wagging vigorously and cats approach mewing a greeting.

Located a short distance both to the south and north of Fataga are camel safari centres, where beasts may be hired for accompanied treks of varying length through the valley.

San Bartolomé de Tirajana

It is possible for those without a hire car to continue by number 18 bus to the not very exciting small town of San Bartolomé de Tirajana (or Tunte), which is encircled by mountains. Although this is the administrative centre of a huge area, including much of the tourist coastline, there is nothing of exceptional architectural interest to be seen. San Bartolomé's church has reopened to visitors after extensive restoration. Roads leading to a *mirador* are signposted, but the views, although pleasant, hardly seem worth a pedestrian's effort. The local *parador*, which has seen better days, even though the food is still quite good, offers a

A roadside shop at San Bartolomé de Tirajana

The road from San Bartolomé de Tirajana to Ayacata crosses the 1,200m high pass of Cruz Grande

splendid view of the Tirajana crater. On the main road, near the bus stop, Bar Martini serves *guindilla*, a local aperitif, which evokes a sweet Fernet Branca. Bar Sergio, nearby, is more adventurous in its selection of *tapas*.

Those returning to San Fernando will approach the end of their hair-raising journey with tranquil views of the Maspalomas coast, dominated by the lighthouse and the sand dunes.

Motorists can continue from San Bartolomé into the high central mountain range of Gran Canaria, an excursion which is described next. Non-motorists wishing to make the same trip have three alternatives: wait until Sunday morning's 8am departure of the 18 bus from San Fernando, travel via Las Palmas or take an escorted tour.

The Central Mountains

Ayacata • Roque Nublo• Roque Bentaiga •Tejeda • Cruz de Tejeda • Los Pichos • Pozo de los Nieves

All those spending their first holiday in Gran Canaria are urged to visit the dramatic range of mountains that occupies most of its centre. Like Tenerife's snow-covered Teide, the range is volcanic in origin, although no similar dramatic cone dominates. This has the visual effect of making Gran Canaria appear to be, erroneously, a larger island than Tenerife, where it is quite difficult to get away from the omnipresent views of its towering mountain. In clear weather, Teide can be seen from much of the north coast and the central mountains of Gran Canaria. Although it rises out of the sea in a faintly menacing way, the volcano now appears to be extinct as its last eruption of any importance was in 1789.

Round-the-island coach tours include the central mountains in their itineraries, and many visitors take advantage of these. There are, however, drawbacks to such tours: most will spend too much time in very touristy restaurants (the price of an indifferent lunch usually being included in the package) and all of them will spend far too much time in souvenir shops, risibly described as *artesanas* (craft shops). Most of these huge emporiums are located far from anywhere of interest, and the poor holidaymaker is trapped — the only alternative is usually to stubbornly remain seated in the coach and read a good book.

Another intrinsic drawback of coach tours, particularly frustrating to photographers, is that stops can be made only where they have been scheduled by the operator, and there are few of them; those travelling by public transport, although dependant on bus stops, will be less retricted.

The weather in the mountains is extremely fickle: on the south coast the sun may well be shining brightly out of a clear blue sky, while mist or torrential rain is blotting out everything from view on the heights, just a few miles distant. In general, a morning start — as early as possible — is recommended, because cloud tends to build up from around mid-day. First, a whispy, inocuous looking white blob makes an appearance in the sky, a few others then form, one of which briefly obscures the sun. The cloud increases, until within an hour there is no blue sky to be seen and the mists descend. Those who have pre-booked either their coach tour or hire car will, of course, have to accept whatever the weather brings but, if at all possible, the mountains should be avoided in overcast conditions, as so little can then be seen. The local radio programme gives weather forecasts in English every morning.

Ayacata

At San Bartolomé de Tirajana, the 815 continues its climb westward towards the island's highest peaks, crossing the pass of Cruz Grande (1,200m, 3,940ft); at Ayacata the road becomes the 811. Nestling at the foot of the mountains, the small village of Ayacata serves as the terminal point for the 18 bus, which leaves San Fernando, Monday to Friday at 11.30am. On Sundays, however, the bus departs much earlier — at 8am — but then, and only then, it continues to Cruz de Tejeda, the best-known viewpoint in the mountain range. It is essential that bus passengers obtain up-to-date information on this route as the service is very infrequent. Set amidst a very rocky terrain, Ayacata is a particularly attractive sight late January to February, when the almond trees are in blossom.

Roque Nublo

Towering high above the village, immediately to the north, at 1,803m (5,914ft) above sea level, Roque Nublo (Cloud Rock), the

Roque Nublo looks down on the neat white town of Tejeda

opposite: Roque Bentaiga dominates the surrounding landscape

loftiest basalt monolith in the world, points skyward from its platform. Although this is not quite the highest point in Gran Canaria, the rock's dramatic appearance has made it the symbol of the island. Some think that Roque Nublo was formed by the Guanches, who appear to have regarded it as sacred, but the shape has been created entirely by climatic erosion. Little vegetation gains a foothold in this rocky landscape, where the effect of wind and rain has created a barren wilderness punctuated by other rock formations, which are similar to, although less dominating than, Roque Nublo's.

Roque Bentaiga

The 811 to Cruz de Tejeda skirts a great plateau after climbing the ridge above Ayacata. To the west can be seen Roque Bentaiga, which motorists may approach more closely by following the track to the left from the point where the main road does an abrupt right turn: there is a car park below it. This monolithic rock was also sacred to the Guanches, many of whom lived in the Guayve caves at its base.

Tejeda

Tejeda nestles in its valley. The attractive village is the terminus for bus 305, operated by Utinsa from Las Palmas via Santa Brígida. Those without their own transport wishing to spend longer in the mountains than the departure time of the last 18 bus to San Fernando permits, may prefer to return to the south coast by this bus (via Las Palmas), leaving Tejeda in the late afternoon — a daily service. Marzipan figures, almonds, honey and *bienmesabes*, a speciality cake, are made and sold in the village, noteworthy outlets for these are Colomar, 129 Calle León y Castillo, and Morales, 4 Calle Viera y Clavijo.

Cruz de Tejeda

Cruz de Tejeda, on a bend in the road 3km (2 miles) north of Tejeda village, is regarded as marking the centre of Gran Canaria. It is so-named from its cross (*cruz*), now of stone but originally made of wood, which stands in the small plaza overlooked by the Parador Nacional de Tejeda. No longer providing overnight accommodation, the *parador*'s bars and restaurant remain open.

The slopes here are heavily wooded with pine trees, but from gaps between them can be gained the most famous view on the island — Roque Bentaiga to the left, and ahead, in the distance, Tenerife's Mount Teide, which gleams spectacularly after a winter snowfall. Unless the weather is poor, many will wish to indulge in a ramble, but remember that Cruz de Tejeda is 1,450m (4,800ft) above sea level, and therefore normally chilly: warm clothing should always be taken as a precaution against abrupt falls in temperature.

Los Pichos

Experienced hikers can, theoretically, treck to the highest point on Gran Canaria, known as Los Pichos (the peaks) or alternatively Pico de las Nueves (Peak of the Snows), at 1,949m (6,393ft) above sea level, but motorists can approach it by road directly from Cruz de Tejeda. The main 811 road is followed eastward (in the direction of Las Palmas) and the first turn right, the 15.3, then taken. At the cross roads turn left on the 18.3 in the direction of Telde and then first right. The entire route cuts through an ancient forest of Canary pines.

Pozo de las Nieves

As a military radio station has been built on Los Pichos, it is more rewarding to continue to the end of the road, which ascends much of the nearby 1,864m (6,114ft) high Pozo de las Nieves: a scramble to the summit is not too difficult. The name of this mountain, meaning Pit of the Snows, is a reference to an ice storage pit that was once excavated on its north side, it has nothing to do with the snows of Tenerife's Mount Teide as many surmise.

For those returning to the south coast, the quickest route is to take the road towards Ayacata, turning left at the cross roads (the 17.6), and then left again, on the 815 to San Bartolomé. If wishing to return to Las Palmas, the right turn at the same cross roads (the 15.3) should be taken; this soon joins the 811, right, to San Mateo, Santa Brígida (see page 160) and Las Palmas.

Running westward from Cruz de Tejeda is a mountain ridge, which descends to the great pine forest of Tamadaba, via Artenara. The road that crosses it, the 17.6, is regarded as one of the most scenic on the island, and should not be missed. Motorists who wish to continue to Tamadaba from Poco de las Nieves should return to the San Mateo/Las Palmas 811 road as described, but then follow it in the opposite direction, turning right at the 17.6 to Artenara. As this excursion is more easily made from Las Palmas, particularly by those using buses, it is described on page 153.

Sioux City

After a 'paella' Western film had been shot on the Cañón del Aguila, a steep-sided ravine running inland from just to the north of San Agustin, it was decided that the set should be retained. This has since been developed as a tourist attraction, and Wild West shows are held.

✳   Sioux City is open most of the day (not Monday), with shows taking place in the square at 12 noon and 6pm. The greatest appeal is to youngsters (plus Wild West enthusiasts), who can enter the village shops, bars, hotel and church. Lunch and dinner are served in the Three Stars Saloon and the BBQ Station. Daytime shows include a bank hold-up, a shootout between villains and the sheriff's men, knife-throwing, lassoing, and cattle-herding in the corrals.

A typical wild-west entertainment, with Can-Can dancers, is presented every Thursday night, and includes a barbecue dinner; this is aimed primarily at adults. Bus 29 runs from Faro de Maspalomas to Sioux City via Playa del Inglés and San Agustín from 11am, but private transport will be needed to return from the Thursday night show.

The Eastern Towns

Lomo de los Letreros •Fortaleza de Ansite • Santa Lucía de Tirajana • Temisas • Agüimes • Barranco de Guayadeque • Ingenio • Telde • Cuatro Puertas • Parque de Cocodrilos • Arinaga
This itinerary keeps just to the east of the high mountains, and includes Telde, Gran Canaria's second largest town. However, those staying at Las Palmas may prefer to visit Telde from there, as it is much nearer and buses are more frequent.

The majority of motorists, and all bus passengers, will start at

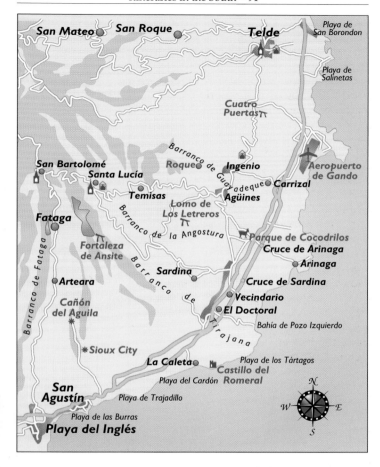

Vecindario, a small town lying on the Carretera del Sur (812), almost precisely between San Agustín and the airport. From here, bus 34 runs to San Bartolomé, via Agüimes.

Lomo de los Letreros
Only very early buses (6.30am) follow a variation to this route, to an ancient Guanche site, via Sardina and Era del Cardón, which

virtually rules it out for those without cars — particularly if the holidaymaker's package includes a hotel breakfast! Motorists taking this alternative route will turn left just before the village of El Doctoral, a short distance south of Vecindario, and follow the Barranco de Tirajana, passing through the village of Sardina (not to be confused with the port of Sardina, at the north-west tip of the island). A right turn at the 815, signposted to Agüimes, leads to the Barranco de la Angostura and the Barranco de Balos, the road crossing both ravines. Overlooking the latter is Lomo de los Letreros, an ancient Guanche site.

Fortaleza de Ansite

A north-westward return by motorists on the 815 passes the end of the road already taken from Sardina, before the northward climb to Santa Lucía is begun. For those with time and a vehicle available, the first left turn off the 815, the 14.4, provides a short detour to Fortaleza de Ansite, believed to mark the last point of Guanche resistance against the Spanish invaders in Gran Canaria. The *fortaleza*, formed of volcanic rock, resembles a fortress, hence its name. It is said that the brave warriors leapt from their 'fortress' at the much better armed Spaniards, shouting their cry of freedom *Atis Tirma*. Every 29 April, Spain's conquest of Gran Canaria in 1483 is celebrated here. The last part of the approach to the rock must be made on foot.

Santa Lucía de Tirajana

A return to the main road soon leads to the agricultural village of Santa Lucía de Tirajana, prettily set on the floor of the Tirajana crater, but no longer consistently tranquil, as it has become a popular halt for coaches, many of which disgorge tourists who will consume lunch at Hao, the village's large restaurant: most eat al fresco from a limited choice menu, the cost of which is generally included in their tour. Those wishing to avoid the crowds are advised to time their visit outside the lunch period. As at nearby San Bartolomé, *guindilla* is a popular aperitif, although not recommended for drivers, due to its high alcohol content.

 Beside the restaurant, the **Museo de la Fortaleza** houses one of the island's best collections of Guanche artefacts. The museum's name does not refer to the Fortaleza de Ansite rock, but to its building's unfortunate, fortress-like exterior, which is not original. The expected examples of pottery, weapons and utensils are displayed, however, the complete skeletons of two Guanches are of greatest interest to most. Simple vegetarian meals similar to those eaten by the Guanches are offered at the museum.

Temisas

Those travelling from Vecindario by the 34 bus will have reached Santa Lucía via Agüimes. Returning bus passengers, as well as motorists driving to Agüimes on the 2.1, will be able to halt at Temisas (or Temises), a charming agricultural village, renowned for its olive production. Caves and burial grounds in the region indicate that this was a popular settlement area for the Guanches. As it is surrounded by olive groves, Temisas is known locally as 'the Jerusalem of the Canaries', however, its houses and winding, cobbled streets are rather more reminiscent of Fataga, which lies about 8km (5 miles) to the southwest.

From Temisas, and also from the 815 road, there are fine views of El Roque, south-east of Agüimes. This rock bastion, although not particularly high, appears quite impressive as it stands proud of the relatively flat surrounding landscape.

Agüimes

Agüimes, 15km (9 miles) from Temisas, boasts an ancient history, but unsympathetic development has meant that, apart from a few houses around its centre, little vernacular architecture of consequence has survived. The church of San Sebastián still manages to impose its great bulk, not only on the town itself, but also on the surrounding countryside. Many are surprised that a town of such modest extent should possess a church so large: the reason is that in the fifteenth century, when San Sebastián was built, Agüimes was the seat of the bishops of the Canary Islands, and continued to be so until the next century.

Barranco de Guayadeque

Only the existence of the intervening ravine appears to have prevented the physical merger of Agüimes with Ingenio, which lies 3km (2 miles) to its north. The ravine's Guanche name,

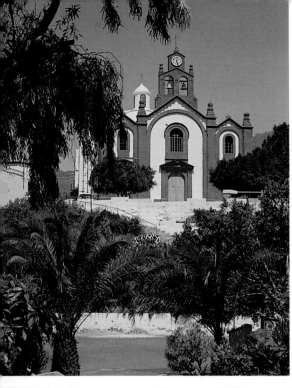

The church of Santa Lucía de Tirajana

El Roque seen from Temisas

The cave dwellings at Roque are now equipped with electricity, television and even street lighting

Guayadeque, means place of flowing water, and water does still flow through it, although now mostly within a conduit. Much of the ravine has been designated a nature reserve.

To reach the valley, take the last turn to the left when leaving Agüimes in the direction of Ingenio; this is only a narrow turning between houses and the Barranco de Guayadeque sign is easily missed. The road is very easy and not particularly steep until its final section. Another road also joins it directly from Ingenio. Picnic sites and parking places are scattered along the valley, which is popular for day trips with the locals, especially at weekends.

 The walls of the ravine contain Guanche caves, some of which are still occupied, and half-way up the valley at **Roque** (not to be confused with the bastion of El Roque to the south-west of Agüimes, or San Roque west of Telde) is a complete village of cave dwellers. At road level there is a church, bar and restaurant all cut into the rock, while a steep path leads to the villagers' cave dwellings above, some with small caves for goats. These rock houses now have electicity and TV aerials, and even 'street' lighting! (Note that on some maps Roque is shown on the wrong road and on the wrong side of the valley.)

At the head of the valley the road passes a large picnic site and then winds steeply to **Montaña de las Tierra**, which comprises no more than a couple of restaurants and a minute chapel. From here there are fine views down into the *barranco*, and walks can be made into the mountains.

Ingenio

Ingenio's wealth was established by the profitable sugar cane, which was grown in plantations around it. Little has survived to indicate the town's former importance, but Ingenio is still regarded as the source of the finest Canarian openwork embroidery to be found on the island. This is perhaps the most attractive souvenir of Gran Canaria with which to return home; generally it is made in the form of napkins, table mats and table cloths. On weekdays, visitors are welcome to observe the traditional skills being taught at the local needlework school. Maria Callas and Aristotle Onassis were famous visitors — yes, they did make purchases.

Immediately north of Ingenio, the 8.1 road towards Carrizal conducts visitors to the **Museo de Piedras** (Rocks Museum) at Las Meijas. In addition to pieces of volcanic rock — mainly varieties of quartz — examples of plants and embroidery are also exhibited, many of which may be purchased. Some will find the old Canary house accommodating the museum as interesting as its collection. It is simple for anyone to reach the museum, as the half-hourly bus 11, Agüimes to Las Palmas, via Ingenio, stops outside.

A return to the 816 junction at Ingenio, followed by a right turn, leads to the large town of Telde, approximately 11km (7 miles) distant. Just over half way along the route, a right turn is signposted to Cuatro Puertas, but this is more conveniently visited on the return journey southward (see page 98). Buses (21, 35, 50) ply along the 816 between Agüimes and Telde fairly regularly.

Telde

Telde is unfairly neglected by most visitors to Gran Canaria. Much of the city is relatively modern and without interest but, unlike Agüimes, the ancient core has been almost completely preserved. Perhaps nowhere else on the island can the thrust of early colonialism be felt so strongly. The Guanches had certainly favoured the area, two of their largest settlements in Gran Canaria, *Tara* and *Cendro*, being located here. It is said that the renowned Guanche ruler, King Doramas, established his court near the present Telde. In the fourteenth century, Telde became the first bishopric in the Canary Islands. Like Agüimes and Ingenio, its wealth had depended on sugar cane, and Telde's economy collapsed when American-produced sugar took over in the mid-sixteenth century: fewer than 1,000 were living in the town by 1700.

The chief monument of Telde is the church of **San Juan Bautista** (St John the Baptist), dating from the late fifteenth century, and still dominating the plaza that bears its name. Externally, the porch is genuine fifteenth-century Gothic work, but the twin towers are relatively modern additions, albeit in the Gothic style.

Internally, the coffered ceilings of the north chapels are

The Barranco de Guayadeque

mudéjar work, a style evolved by Moorish Christian 'converts' in Spain. It is known that Moors were among those engaged in the arduous work of cane-cutting at Telde, and they may have influenced this feature.

The pointed arch of the chancel is a rare late-Gothic example in the islands. Within the chancel are two of the most important artistic treasures to be found in the Canaries. Embellishing the high altar is a figure of Christ, sculpted from the compressed leaves and roots of maize; it is attributed to the skill of Mexican Indians from the state of Tabasco. Even more important, to the south of this, displayed within an enormous glass case, is a carved and gilded wooden altarpiece, which is contemporary with the church. This was purchased in Flanders (at the time annexed by Spain) by Cristóbal García de Castillo, who had been one of the military leaders instrumental in subjugating the Guanches in Gran Canaria. He presented the carving to the church, and apparently it had to be divided into two sections, which were brought to Gran Canaria from Flanders in separate ships. The carved panels depict Nativity scenes.

Of greatest appeal to most tourists visiting Telde, however, is its **San Francisco Quarter**. This is best approached from Calle Carlos E Navarro, a picturesque street running off the town's principal thoroughfare. Whitewashed houses, exposed stone-work around doors and windows, and pitched roofs evoke an ancient village. Most roads are cobbled, and wind tortuously up the slopes of the low hill on which the quarter is built. A sense of peace and calm prevails, particularly around the **convent and church of San Francisco**. The latter now serves as a venue for exhibitions and concerts, entry being dependant on the event being staged. Although no fittings of interest are to be seen, the coffered ceiling may still be admired.

A Spanish Foreign Minister, Fernando León y Castillo (1842-1918) was born and lived in Telde at 43 Calle León y Castillo. His house, now the **Casa Museo de Fernando León y Castillo**, is open to visitors. Personal memorabilia is displayed, together with León y Castillo's large collection of books.

Cuatro Puertas & Carrizal
Some may wish to continue from Telde to Las Palmas, just 13km

to the north, and the city is described in the following chapter. Those returning southward from Telde, however, will follow the 816 as far as its junction with the 812, which heads eastward to the airport. A short distance along the 812 rises the Montaña Sagrado de Cuatro Puertas (Sacred Mountain of the Four Gateways). It is believed that members of the Guanche parliament, known as the Tagoror, assembled before the mountain's great megalith. This was regarded as sacred, and religious ceremonies are also likely to have been held around it. Traces of decoration remain within some of the mountain's Guanche caves.

The hourly 36 bus from Telde to Faro de Maspalomas stops at Cuatro Puertas, and then continues southward on the 812 (Carretera del Sur) to Carrizal, where those who have not already seen needleworkers exhibiting their skills may wish to visit the Artesanía La Molina. From Carrizal, the 36 bus continues southward to Cruce de Arinaga, a major crossroads, from where the 02 bus from the southern resorts follows the 2.3 westward to Parque de Cocodrilos, at Los Corralillos, to which many will wish to allocate several hours. Alternatively, the 22 bus (starting at Agüimes) continues eastward along the 815 to the fishing port of Arinaga (see below).

Parque de Cocodrilos (Crocodile Park)

In spite of its name, this park has much more to offer than its collection of more than 250 crocodiles. There are three sections: a general zoo (including tigers, bears and monkeys), tropical plants and birds, and a series of crocodile ponds. A programme of free shows is held every day, in addition to the expected feeding of crocodiles. Included are: flamenco dancing, performing parrots, acrobatics and *paella* making. Loudspeakers throughout the park give advance notice of each show. Recently added to the complex is a high-technology 3D cinema: only in Japan, at the time of writing, is there a similar example.

The 02 bus returns to the southern resorts from the park, following the *carretera*. Motorists are able to join the *Autoroute* at exit 3.

Arinaga

Although not outstandingly picturesque, Arinaga is the only

coastal village of any size in the south-east to have escaped tourist development, and it retains a genuine Canary ambience: there are good *tapas* bars and several fish restaurants, a few of which overlook the promenade that skirts the dark-sand beach. As may be expected, prices here are much lower than in the resorts, and few tourists will be seen. At the end of the jetty, a small lighthouse, while in no way rivalling that of Las Maspalomas, emphasises Arinaga's maritime location.

Between this port and Las Palmas there are numerous small beaches, that of **El Hombre** having been adopted in the winter by Swedes, but none is really worth a special visit by those with limited time at their disposal: they are best left to the local families. From the *carretera* it is a short drive southward to San Agustín, and back to the world of international tourism.

Additional Information

Eating Out
Acaymo
Carretera de Mogán
Valle de Mogán
☎ 74 02 63
Open: 12 noon-11.30pm (not Mondays)

Places to Visit
Gran Karting (Go carts)
Carretera del Sur
Tarajalillo
☎ 76 00 90
Open: Summer 11am-10pm, winter 100am-9pm

Mundo Aborigen
Carretera de Fataga
Open: daily 10am-6pm

Palmitos Park
Barranco de Chamoriscán
Open: daily 9am-6pm

Parque de Cocodrilos
Los Coralillos
Open: Sunday-Friday 10am-6pm

Sioux City
Cañón del Aguila
☎ 76 25 73
Open 10am-8pm (shows at 12 noon and 6pm)
Barbecue/dinner Thursdays at 8pm

Telde
Casa Museo de Fernando León y Castillo
43 Calle Calle León y Castillo
Open: Monday-Friday 9am-2pm
Admission free.

Gleaming ceramic tiles on a cafe in Parque de San Telmo,
designed in Spanish Modernist style

opposite: a leafy square in the Triana quarter of Las Palmas

Las Palmas

4

No first-time visitor to the island should neglect to spend some time in Las Palmas, the largest and most important city in the archipelago. Those arriving in Gran Canaria on a flight-only basis will be able to decide at the very last moment whether or not to head immediately for the city, rather than the southern resorts, as they will have had an up-to-date view of the weather just prior to landing at Gando airport. Fortunately, not even the power of the alleged taxi 'mafia' has been able to stop the direct Salcai bus 60 running from the airport to Las Palmas, 22 km (14 miles) distant, every 30 minutes throughout most of the day.

Day-trippers to Las Palmas from the southern resorts are provided with several bus services, but the 30, which runs every 20 minutes, is direct and by far the quickest. The others, includ ing the 05 night bus, stop everywhere. Note that at the time of writing the last 30 leaves Las Palmas from the Estación de Guaguas in Parque de San Telmo at 8.50pm.

Although a street plan of Las Palmas gives the impression that the city is formidably extensive, for tourists it is really quite small, as only four easily-managed sections, each of which borders the sea, will be of much interest to them. The most appealing sector architecturally is undoubtedly the old part of the city, formed by the Triana and Vegueta quarters. Second in importance is the Las Canteras Beach area, where most visitors stay. A brief, uninteresting stretch between Parque de Santa Catalina, just south of Canteras, leads to the city's great shopping thoroughfare, Avenida de Mesa y Lopez, along which the large stores are grouped. Bisecting the long stretch between the old city and the great shops is Parque Doramas, which those with sufficient time available may like to visit, as it incorporates the Museo de Néstor in the Pueblo Canario and the Hotel de Santa Catalina, the oldest-established luxury hotel in the city.

Holidaymakers seeking hotels in Las Palmas generally prefer to stay near the magnificent Las Canteras beach, and to reach them, municipal buses 1 or 12 to Parque Santa Catalina or Puerto should be taken. Both leave from Avenida Rafael Cabrera (but at different stops), directly outside the bus station (Estación de Guaguas) — ask the driver to halt as near as possible to the street required. If seeking budget accommodation, the best area to make for is the north end of Las Canteras, in the side streets of which clean and comfortable *hostals* and *pensiones* may be found. The Mercado de Puerto bus stop is more convenient for this area.

For day visitors from the south wishing to see the most picturesque sector of Las Palmas, the Parque de San Telmo, which faces the bus station, is conveniently located to begin a tour on foot.

The majority of motorists that have hired a car for their entire holiday will understandably drive to Las Palmas, but, as in most of the world's large cities, parking can be difficult and, once the car has been parked, it will prove much easier to tour the old quarter on foot, returning to the vehicle later, perhaps for the fairly lengthy drive to Las Canteras.

As Las Palmas is approached, the truncated tower of the

Castillo de San Cristóbal is passed, overlooking the sea on the
right-hand side. At the point where the motorway crosses the
Guineguada ravine there are excellent views, to the left, of the
ancient Vegueta quarter of the city, dominated by its great
cathedral.

Triana Quarter

The Triana quarter of Las Palmas gained its name in the early
sixteenth century, when many Spaniards emigrated to it from
the Triana sector of Seville — perhaps they became homesick?
At that time, the quarter, which is located immediately north of
the Barranco de Guiniguada, was very much the working class
area of Las Palmas, the higher orders preferring to live south of
the ravine, in Vegueta, away from the noise and refuse associated with the port. It was in Triana that English and Scots first
settled early in the nineteenth century, when the British began to
establish trading companies in Las Palmas.

   Parque de San Telmo marks the northern border of Triana, its
splendid trees providing shelter on sunny days for city centre
workers. In the north-west corner of the park stands a recently-
restored kiosk which, although tiny, is not exceeded in charm by
any other building in the city. The kiosk was designed simply to
serve as a café, which it still does, and is a superb example of
Spanish Modernism, a style developed by Gaudí and his con-
temporaries in Barcelona, where the finest examples are to be
found. Particularly effective are the glazed tiles that almost
cover the building. Don Rafael Masanet Farns was the architect,
and the kiosk was completed as recently as 1923. A bandstand in
the park has been renovated recently.

   In the south-west corner of the park, the small **Ermita de San
Telmo**, built in the fifteenth century as a hermitage, is the second
oldest church in Gran Canaria. Formerly, the sea almost lapped
its sanctuary, but land has since been reclaimed. Internally, the
roof of the building and the sanctuary's east wall are of wood,
the latter being painted in the sixteenth century. However, San
Telmos's most important fitting is its baroque reredos, made in
1766. On the waterfront nearby, shortly after the hermitage had
been built, the first port in Las Palmas was established by the

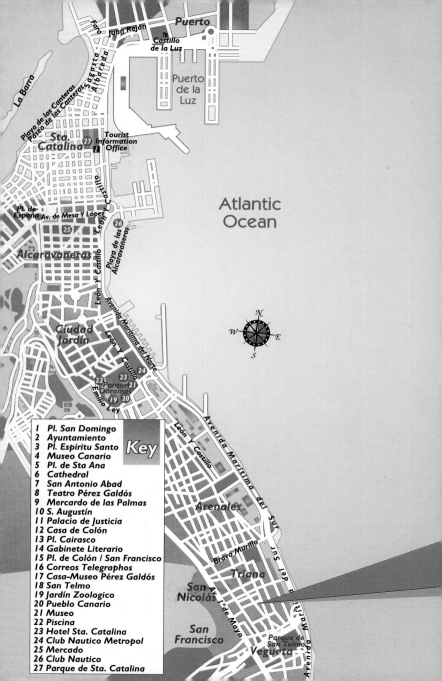

Puerto

Faro

Juan Rejón

Castillo
de la Luz

Sagasta

Albareda

La Barra

Playa de las Canteras

Paséo de las Canteras

**Puerto
de la
Luz**

**Sta.
Catalina**

27

**Tourist
Information
Office**

Pl. de
España

Av. de Mesa Y López

25

26

Alcaravaneras

León Y Castillo

León Y Castillo

Playa de las Alcaravaneras

**Atlantic
Ocean**

**Ciudad
Jardín**

León Y Castillo

Avenida Marítima del Norte

N

W E

S

22

23 24

19 20

21

**Parque
Doramas**

Emilio Ley

León Y Castillo

Avenida Marítima del Sur

Key

1 Pl. San Domingo
2 Ayuntamiento
3 Pl. Espiritu Santo
4 Museo Canario
5 Pl. de Sta Ana
6 Cathedral
7 San Antonio Abad
8 Teatro Pérez Galdós
9 Mercardo de las Palmas
10 S. Augustín
11 Palacio de Justicia
12 Casa de Colón
13 Pl. Cairasco
14 Gabinete Literario
15 Pl. de Colón / San Francisco
16 Correos Telegraphos
17 Casa-Museo Pérez Galdós
18 San Telmo
19 Jardín Zoologico
20 Pueblo Canario
21 Museo
22 Piscina
23 Hotel Sta. Catalina
24 Club Nautico Metropol
25 Mercado
26 Club Nautico
27 Parque de Sta. Catalina

Arenales

Bravo Murillo

Triana

**San
Nicolás**

San
de Mayo

**San
Francisco**

Vegueta

Parque de
San Telmo

Avenida Marítima

Las Palmas

construction of a jetty, and sailors soon adopted the hermitage for their worship.

On the west side of the Parque de San Telmo stands the former Canary Island headquarters of the Spanish army, from where Franco proclaimed his opposition to the Republican government on 18 July 1936, thereby setting in motion the Spanish Civil War: a plaque commemorates the occasion.

Calle Mayor de Triana, now pedestrianized and paved with granite, is the most important shopping street in the old city. Those staying in Gran Canaria over the Christmas period will be able to admire its renowned decorations. Would-be purchasers should bear in mind that virtually all the shopkeepers are enthusiastic followers of the siesta, and few remain open during 1-4pm. If afternoon shopping is planned, it will be necessary to visit Avenida de Mesa y López in the Alcaravaneras quarter (see page 131), where all the shops, including the city's main department stores, remain open. To recommend specific shops from the many in Calle Mayor de Triana is an invidious task, but those in search of duty-free articles can be recommended to visit the prestigious Maya, on the west side of the street (Parque de San Telmo end) at number 7.

Many popular *tapas* bars are to be found in Triana, most of them lying in the side streets to the north of Calle Mayor de Triana. Calle Perdomo, the third turning right, has two of interest: Yurfa, with occasional live music and art exhibitions, is set in a grand, early nineteenth-century house built for a British resident of Las Palmas; Factoría, nearby, is, in contrast, ultra-modern and fashionable with younger people.

As with most shopping streets, the shopfronts in Calle Mayor de Triana give little clue to the age of the properties, but a glance above ground floor level indicates the variety of styles employed, dating from the sixteenth to the twentieth centuries. At the far end of the street, on the left, is a particularly attractive group of Modernist houses, built in the 1920s and incorporating colourful ceramic tiles. Calle Torres, fourth right after returning from Calle Perdomo to Calle Mayor de Triana, leads to Calle Cano, first left.

On the left, at number 6, is **Casa-Museo Pérez Galdós**. Here was born, on 10 May 1843, the Canary Islands' most famous novelist, Benito Pérez Galdós. The writer, who like his English contemporary Charles Dickens, exposed social injustices, spent much of his life in Madrid and Santander, and furniture from his properties there is exhibited, including the bed in which he died, on 18 January 1920. Of particular interest is the dining room suite, embellished with ceramics, which was designed by Galdós himself for his house in Madrid.

Although, naturally, the museum has the greatest appeal to Spaniards, entrance is free and provides an opportunity for all to view the interior of a typical nineteenth-century Las Palmas town house, together with its furnishings.

Calle Cano leads to Calle Peregrina where, at number 7, Bar Peregrina incorporates one of the most popular al fresco cafés in Triana. At the south end of the street, a right turn at Calle Remedios leads to the small but charming **Plaza de Cairasco**, the name of which commemorates a nineteenth-century Canary poet.

On the north side of this square is another delightful Modernist building, the **Gabinete Literario**, gleaming with ceramics. Modern works of art by Canarios are frequently on view within this 'literary library'.

Still overlooking the square is the former Hotel Madrid, where Franco was residing at the outbreak of the Civil War, on 17 July 1936.

Calle General Bravo, to the west, separates the plaza from La Alameda (the tree-lined avenue), a small park, originally encircled by railings. In 1892, the 400th anniversary of Christopher Columbus's voyage of discovery to the New World, a commemorative bust of the explorer was erected on a plinth at the north end of the park. Since then, this popular green space, rare in the old quarter of the city, has been popularly known as **Plaza de Colón**.

Occupying the north end of the plaza is the great façade of **San Francisco**, a convent church built in the fifteenth century. Roads southward lead to the Barranco de Guiniguada, which has been partly filled to accommodate a dual carriageway, Carretera Tafira, but was formerly a deep ravine (as it still is further inland), crossed by several bridges.

Remaining on the Triana side, an attractive promenade may

Calle Mayor de Triana decorated for Christmas

Modernist architecture above the shop fronts in Calle Mayor de Triana

be followed seaward towards the Avenida Marítima del Sur, which performs a serpentine, multi-level split, prohibiting any maritime views. At the lower end of the promenade, commemorating the site of Puente Palo, the 'commercial' bridge across the ravine, which formerly linked Triana and Vegueta, a delightful, ceramic-faced box screens a duct. On this is reproduced a pictorial map of the ancient area around the bridge.

The south-east corner of Triana is marked by the **Teatro Pérez Galdós**, built in Modernist style in 1919. This theatre was, of course, named to commemorate the novelist, whose house has been described. Its 'season' is the winter, when concerts, opera and ballet are performed. Most of the theatre's decoration is the work of the renowned Canary painter and sculptor Néstor Martín Fernández de la Torre (1887-1938), who worked primarily in Madrid and Paris, but was always influenced by Canary traditions. It is usually possible to view the great foyer, where the decorative theme (including the carved balustrades) is Canary flora.

The theatre is the starting point (Teatro) for many Las Palmas bus routes, which depart from its seaward side. Just west of the theatre's façade, the dual carriageway may be crossed with safety to Vegueta.

Vegueta Quarter

The Vegueta quarter is where Las Palmas was founded in the fifteenth century, and where most of the city's ancient buildings are located. Vegueta means a small area of flat land, and in extent it is little more than a village, albeit a very grand village. On approaching Las Palmas from the south, via the elevated Avenida Marítima del Sur, it will have become dramatically apparent that the cathedral still dominates the Vegueta skyline, confirming the caring preservation of the quarter by the municipal authorities.

It is known that the slopes of the Barranco Guiniguada, which bisects the old city, were formerly studded with palm trees, and this is how Las Palmas gained its name: none of the trees has survived, nor has any trace of the sixteenth-entury wall that once protected the Vegueta and Triana quarters to the north and south. This wall, erected originally for defence reasons, was kept so that taxes could be levied on goods entering or leaving the city; it was finally demolished in the nineteenth century.

Skirting the Mercado Municipal de Las Palmas is Calle Mendizábal, formerly known as Calle General Mola. Following the restoration of democracy in Spain, most streets that had been re-named to honour Franco and his generals reverted to their original name (in Triana, for example, the important Avenida Generalissimo Franco became Avenida 1⁰ de Mayo). Some current street maps of Las Palmas have still not caught up with these changes.

The **Mercado Municipal** of Vegueta is the city's longest estab-   ※
lished and most important market. By tradition, the forty stalls originally led to its being known, cynically, as 'the Market of the Forty Thieves'. Notwithstanding, the prices are now very reasonable, and this is a good place in which to buy charcuterie, cheese and fruit for a picnic lunch. Those unable to visit the small town of Guía, in the north of the island, may wish to buy some *queso de Guía*, a cheese that is unusually flavoured with wild flowers, a Canary speciality. Set in the sides of the market building are a multitude of tiny, economically-priced bars. Outside the market small groups of men may be seen discussing the merits of the canaries that are offered for sale in small cages.

Further down the same street, at 5-7, is a Las Palmas institution, El Herreño, specializing in Canarian dishes served either at the restaurant's large bar or in the dining room. Hierro is the least-visited of all the Canary Islands, but it appears to have a tradition of good food, as many of the restaurants in Las Palmas, like this one, are owned by Herreños. Cheese and cheesecake from the island of Hierro is a speciality, which can be found in Las Palmas.

Calle Mendizábal continues southward to Calle Roque Morera. This street, together with its continuation, **Calle de los Balcones**, is one of the most picturesque in Gran Canaria. At its west end, closing the vista, is the rear of the cathedral. Calle de los Balcones is still shown on many maps as Calle León y Joven, its former name. Presumably, it was rechristened to emphasize the tourist appeal of the street's splendid balconies (*balcones*).

Photographers attempting to obtain an atmospheric shot of

the street are now rather frustrated by the promotional banners that are unsympathetically and permanently hung outside the eighteenth-century façade of the **Centro Atlantico de Arte Moderno** (CAAM) building, half way up the street at numbers 9-11. Frequently changing exhibitions may be viewed in its modern interior.

Running southward from Calle Roque Morera, Calle San Agustín leads to the small **church of San Agustín**, with its bell tower. Adjacent, overlooking the sea, is the **Palacio de Justicia**, which accommodates Gran Canaria's Law Courts.

Return to Calle Mendizábal and turn first left, following Calle Montes de Oca. At number 10, Restaurante Montesdeoca is the prettiest eating place in Las Palmas. It was opened in 1990 in a grand colonial house built in 1515; many will wish to dine al fresco in its cool, galleried patio, fish being the speciality.

Just past the restaurant, where the road opens out to form a plaza, stands the small church or hermitage (Ermita) of **San Antonio Abad**. This was the first church founded in Las Palmas, but the present structure dates from the complete rebuilding of 1892, another Las Palmas commemoration of the discovery of America. It is believed that Christopher Columbus would have heard Mass in the original church, on Sunday 26 August 1492, during his brief stay on the island, as recorded on the plaque. An extraordinary display of bougainvillaea embellishes the exterior of the building — a delight for photographers. Within, all is nineteenth-century baroque.

Casa Museo de Colón (Columbus Museum)

Streets around the church are narrow and short, but clearly identified. The cobbled Pasaje Pedro de Algaba runs southward from Plaza de San Antonio Abad, curving around the most famous secular building in the Canary Islands, the Casa-Museo de Colón. (Note that the entrance is at the side of the building, not the door facing the rear of the cathedral.) This late fifteenth-century house was probably built specifically for the island's first Spanish governor, Pedro de Vera, who was certainly residing here in 1482. In the logbook of his flagship *Santa María*, Christopher Columbus records that he landed at Las Palmas on 25 August 1492 for minor repairs to be made to his other two caravels. He stayed until 1 September and, due to the royal patronage he had obtained, it is assumed that the explorer would have been accommodated in the governor's residence. However, as was common with many important events concerning Columbus, this is conjecture. During his second and fourth voyages to America, in 1493 and 1502 respectively, Columbus also stayed for brief periods on the island.

The two-storey complex of buildings making up the museum rambles around galleried patios, its chief architectural features being carved doorways, arches and window surrounds in the Isabelline style. Unique to Spain, the name of the style commemorates Queen Isabel (or Isabella) I, with whom it is contemporary; its most distinctive feature is profuse sculptural detail applied to Gothic forms, similar in spirit to the almost contemporary Tudor Renaissance work in England.

Following the building's conversion to a museum, items were assembled here from all the Canaries appertaining to the early history of the islands. The main patio is four-sided, and accommodates canons, an eighteenth-century wine vat and an Italian

The tranquil Plaza del Pilar Nuevo and the façade of the Casa de Colón

marble font from San Antonio Abad. Painted on the patio's walls are the routes followed by Columbus to the Canary Islands during his first, second and fourth voyages to America.

Linked with the main patio is the three-sided Patio de Armas (Arms), so-named because the ceremony of the governor's guard presenting arms took place here. The central well is contemporary with it. From a third patio, steps ascend to the upper galleries.

Furniture, engravings and paintings are displayed throughout the museum. In room 202, there are replicas of *Santa María*, *La Pinta* and *La Niña*, the three caravels that represented the small fleet of Columbus on his first voyage to America; wall maps trace the explorer's four expeditions to the New World. It is interesting to reflect that when Columbus first landed in Gran Canaria, the nearby islands of Tenerife and La Palma were still ruled by Guanches.

In room 206, a model of the Castillo de la Luz in its original form (see page 125), shows that it was formerly surrounded by water. In the museum there is a crypt, not always open, with a timber ceiling in which the tombstone of a Guanche princess is displayed.

Another splendid mansion, the **Casa de los Hidalgos**, a nobleman's nineteenth-century residence, adjoins the Casa de Colón.

On leaving the museum, a left turn leads to the rear of the cathedral, overlooking Plaza del Pilar Nuevo. To the south, this plaza has swallowed up all of Calle Francisco María de León and part of Calle Felipe Massieu Falcon, the names of which can still be seen displayed on walls. It seems likely that houses in these streets formerly clustered around the cathedral in a medieval European manner before being cleared for the plaza.

Catedral de Santa Ana & Museo de Arta Sacro

Continue to 20 Calle Espiritu Santo, which skirts the south side of the cathedral, and provides entry to it via the Museo de Arte Sacro (Museum of Sacred Art). The cathedral may only be entered free of charge (from its west front) by those attending Mass, and no tours of the building are then permitted.

Many of the exhibits in the Museum of Sacred Art are early American work, some executed by Aztec converts to Christianity. Pre-eminent is an enamelled gold monstrance, attributed to Benvenuto Cellini. Unfortunately, the cathedral's most treasured possession, the fifteenth-century Pendón de la Conquista (Banner of the Conquest), traditionally embroidered personally by Queen Isabella I, is too valuable for permanent display, and may be seen only on special occasions.

Entered from the museum is the Capilla de los Dolores, in the south-east corner of the cathedral. Displayed here, within a glass coffin, is the well-preserved body of the revered Bishop (Obispo) Codina, of the Canaries, who died in 1857; one wonders if this was a conscious revival of the mummifications once practised by the Guanches.

The Cathedral of Santa Ana was founded in 1497, but not completed in its present form until 1915. Internally, the building is late Gothic with Renaissance elements, while the west façade (seen later) owes its baroque appearance primarily to the eighteenth century. A nave and its flanking north and south aisles, all of the same height, give the appearance of a triple-naved interior. Small windows allow very little natural light, and the cathedral is undoubtedly gloomy.

Ribs from the slender columns explode into delicate 'palm' vaults, reminiscent of fan-vaulting, a purely English architectural feature. The Plateresque style of the columns exhibits filigree carving, which evokes the work of silversmiths (*plata* = silver), hence the name of the style. Gothic, Renaissance, and even Moorish themes were incorporated in Plateresque, which was restricted to Spain, and only appeared in the early sixteenth century as a development of the Isabelline style: examples in the Canaries are few.

Marauding Dutch sailors robbed the cathedral of its finest works of art before setting fire to the building in the sixteenth century, a particularly grievous loss being the carved reredos of the high altar; due to this, Santa Ana's artistic treasures are few. Paintings on the whole are rather dull, the best being those of the Virgin and Saint Sebastian, above the sanctuary doors in the east wall, the work of the island's finest eighteenth-century painter, Juan de Miranda. A statue of the Virgin, by José Luján Pérez, one of the Canario's most important works, is displayed at the north end of the sanctuary.

After leaving the cathedral and its museum, continue west-ward along Calle Espiritu Santo to **Plaza de Santa Ana**, the most important square in Las Palmas. In spite of its classical appearance, the dimensions of the plaza and the functions of the buildings around it have altered little in almost 500 years. It is here that celebrations of major events still take place. At Corpus Christi, each May, the paving of the Plaza de Santa Ana is decorated with flowers, laid out in formal patterns.

As usual, the west front was the last major part of the cathedral to be constructed: virtually all important churches are begun at the east (sanctuary) end so that services may be held before the building is finished. From its appearance, the façade is of eighteenth- or early nineteenth-century design, the exuberant roofline, the balustrades and the pepperpot cupolas of the twin towers being typically baroque features. Rather surprising is the central rose window, the revival of a feature from medieval Gothic architecture.

The dullness of the stone, which would be partly alleviated by cleaning, is reduced when the afternoon sun strikes this side of the building. Apparently, the exterior of the cathedral remains unfinished. Those attending Mass enter from the west façade; no other building in the plaza is open to visitors.

Facing the cathedral are two pairs of bronze dogs, a reference to the huge wild dogs recorded on the islands in early times. It is not known what they looked like, and each of the four depict different breeds — the sculptor hoping, perhaps, that by the law of averages one would be approximately accurate. All possess noble expressions, and Landseer might well have been proud to have cast them. The Canary Islands owe their name to these extinct dogs (*canis* being Latin for dogs) and they have been represented in the coat of arms of the islands since 1506.

On the north side of the plaza is the **Palacio Episcopal**, the seat of the bishops of the Canary Islands for many centuries. Although its patio is not open, glimpses may be obtained of the pine door surrounds and balconies typical of the early buildings of the Vegueta.

The **Ayuntamiento** (City Hall) faces the cathedral from the west end of th plaza. It has been here since the sixteenth century, but the present building is mid-nieteenth-century work.

Known as **Casa Regental** (Regent's House), the building on the south side of the plaza was formerly the headquarters of the Spanish forces that guarded the islands. The Inquisition was established in the square in the sixteenth century.

Plaza Espiritu Santo opens out to the south of the Ayuntamiento, its tiny hermitage church having stood for many centuries on the corner with Calle Espiritu Santo.

The baroque west façade of the Catedral de Santa Ana

From the south-west corner of the plaza, Calle Luis Millares runs southward to join **Plaza Santo Domingo**, overlooked by its monastic church of the same name. A return northward ends at Calle Doctor Chil, right, with the Museo Canario at number 25.

Museo Canario

Established in the nineteenth century, exhibits in the Museo Canario include geology, pre-history and history; there is also an extensive library and a map collection. Those who have visited Mundo Aborigen, in the south of the island, will be particularly fascinated by exhibits relating to the Guanches, which form the bulk of the collection. Unfortunately, captions are in Spanish only, and those without a reasonable standard of Spanish are advised to bring a pocket dictionary.

In addition to skeletons and skulls, some of which indicate violent deaths, there are, on the upper floor, a large number of mummies in varying states of preservation, wrapped in goat hides. Guanche utensils, figurines and ceramics demonstrate the artistic abilities of the native people. Included are mysterious-looking wedge-shaped blocks with grooves on one side, known as *pintaderas*; possibly they were used as seals or even, it has been suggested, for tatooing. Most that have been discovered are of terracotta, but wooden and stone examples also exist.

Of great interest is a reproduction of the famous cave at Gáldar, the Cueva Pintada, with its Guanche wall paintings. The cave has been closed to the public for conservation work since 1970 (see page 141).

Contemporary topographical illustrations of Canary Island towns in the late sixteenth century are an invaluable and fascinating record. Equally invaluable are the library's copies of newspapers published in the Canaries since the late eighteenth century.

Further down Calle Doctor Chil, at number 17, is the **Seminario Concilia**, founded here in 1777. A plaque records that this was the Ancient College of Jesuits, presented by Carlos III. Its courtyard was restored in 1993. The Jesuit church of the college is typically baroque, its doorway flanked by twisted 'barleysugar' columns.

All the streets leading northward from Calle Doctor Chil

return to the dual carriageway separating Vegueta from Triana. From the seaward side of Teatro Pérez Galdós, several buses commence their journeys northward. Most visitors will now wish to continue to Parque de Santa Catalina, a short distance from Las Canteras Beach, and reached by buses 1, 12, 22 and 41. Bus number 1, although slower, is more frequent than the others; it follows Calle León y Castillo, the main north/south artery of Las Palmas, for its entire length. Those who prefer to visit Parque Doramas (see page 133) first, followed by the department stores in Avenida de Mesa y López, may stop off on route.

Santa Catalina Quarter

Parque de Santa Catalina is undoubtedly the most popular Las Palmas venue for al fresco café life. In recent years, its fashionable status became somewhat diminished by the drop-outs, alcoholics, drug adicts, vagrants and prostitutes who had taken to congregating on its benches, but strenuous efforts have been made to overcome this problem, aided by a costly improvement scheme. The main road, which formerly bisected the park, has been sunk below it, and the buildings on the waterfront side refurbished and converted to cultural purposes. Throughout this turmoil, the city's **Tourist Information Office** (Casa de Turismo), in its Canary-style building, remained open. Jet-foil ferries linking Gran Canaria with the other Canary Islands dock beside the park, and passengers are now presented with a much more attractive introduction to the city than before.

Most buildings on the west side of the park accommodate a bar on the ground floor, with its associated restaurant separated by a public walkway. The dining areas are open to the sky, but may be covered rapidly if the weather turns showery. Menus appear to be similar, concentrating on international dishes, as might be expected. Towards the centre, the adjoining bars of Derby and Rio are favoured by the gay community.

Located in the north-east corner, at 6 Calle de Luis Morote, is the **British Consulate**, which will help British holidaymakers in ✳ an emergency. Behind the park, the buildings are divided between the red-light district operators and duty-free shops selling a bewildering range of cameras, watches and audio equipment: the prices first quoted (both by the importuning girls and the shop assistants) are rarely those eventually paid. Worth visiting, particularly by cigar smokers, is Tabaquería Bazar Marquez, in Calle Ripoche, which runs westward from the centre of the park. Here can be found the finest Palmitos, acclaimed cigars from the nearby island of La Palma.

Playa de Las Canteras (Las Canteras Beach) — Northern Section

Calle General Vives runs directly behind the cafés of Parque de Santa Catalina, interconnecting at its east end with Calle de Sagasta, which continues northward, many of its stores maintaining the city's duty-free theme. After four blocks have been passed, however, all thoughts of shopping will be abruptly dispelled, as the buildings end and Paseo de las Canteras is joined, open to the sea, and presenting the visitor with a heart-stopping sight — Las Canteras Beach.

Few of the world's great cities possess a beach at all, let alone a natural beach of golden sand, protected by an off-shore barrier of rocks and almost enclosed by romantic, verdant mountains. It seems strange, therefore, that the international fame of Playa de Las Canteras is not more widespread — indeed, many holiday-makers leave Gran Canaria completely ignorant of its existence.

Nowhere else in the Canary Islands is there a beach that is remotely comparable. Set in a great horseshoe bay open to the west, the open sea is hidden from much of Las Canteras, suggesting that the beach fringes a lake rather than the Atlantic Ocean. Due to the intervening mountains, Las Canteras, unlike the Costa Canaria resorts, suffers little from strong winds, and the water is often significantly warmer because, at low tide, the protective reef creates what is virtually a shallow lagoon. This reef, *La Barra*, is composed of a rare type of rock, known as *canteras*, which has given the beach its name. In a poll taken recently, Las Canteras was voted among the top ten most beautiful beaches in the world. Since then, its promenade, Paseo de las Canteras, has been completely remodelled (with the help of EU grants), significantly improving its amenities. By 1995, the entire 2½ mile stretch had been completed.

Why then can this great beach be almost deserted when the outstretched bodies of sunbathing holidaymakers leave barely a

*Unoccupied sunbeds await early sunbathers at La Canteras beach,
with the mountains of the north coast in the background*

*Some bathers share the beach with fishing boats for added protection
from breezes*

grain of sand visible at Puerto Rico, a few miles to the south? The answer, of course, is the difference in sunshine hours, which is caused by the moist air carried by the prevailing north-east trade winds rising as the mountains are reached and forming clouds. Nevertheless, when the air pressure is high ,or the wind is in the south-east, Las Canteras can be blessed with days on end of cloudless blue skies; the problem is that such periods cannot be accurately predicted, even though locals recommend March, September and October as the best time.

Calle de Sagasta runs parallel with Paseo de Las Canteras for several blocks, but most will wish to ascend immediately to the slightly raised promenade. This is the northern end of Playa de Las Canteras, the liveliest sector of the beach, and from where the finest views are obtained. Only here are the local fishermen permitted to beach their boats, and the more mature local residents seem to favour this stretch, laying out their towels and sunbeds between the vessels, thus gaining added protection from any passing breezes, most of which blow down the approach roads to the beach rather than from the sea. At this point, the promenade does an abrupt left turn before finally petering out into a short headland, known as La Puntilla (the Little Point).

Bearing in mind the perpetual mildness of the climate, it is a surprise to find Peridis, at 6 Paseo de las Canteras, with its vast stock of fur coats. The absence of duty evidently makes them a bargain for overseas visitors.

Many bars and fish speciality restaurants are to be found on this part of the promenade but, sadly, the days of the 'shack' bar, located on La Puntilla, appear to be numbered, as redevelopment is planned. In 1995, there was talk of a nautical school and shops being constructed on the headland, grouped around a plaza, but the locals are sceptical that it will ever be built. If possible, get to the 'shack' bar before it finally closes, there is surely nowhere else in Las Palmas, possibly the world, where a triple Gordons gin (distilled in London, not Málaga) and Schweppes tonic can be purchased for less than 200 pesetas — the superb view, observed from tables and chairs, is free.

Just off the beach, in side streets such as Calle La Naval, low-cost *hostal* accommodation and *pensiones* with private shower and toilet, can still be found. However, if any sleep during the night is anticipated, insist on a rear room overlooking the lightwell of the building. Practically every street in this quarter is packed with bars and discos which, until the early hours of the morning, emit music at full blast, as much to lure in passers by as to entertain their customers.

Lovers of coffee drowned in alcohol may like to try the many varieties dreamed up at La Posada, 8 Calle Naval. An incredibly good value bar/restaurant, Hesperides, is to be found nearby, at 63 Calle Sagasta.

La Isleta

Streets running north from Calle La Naval lead to La Isleta, the port workers' area. It is said that long ago this was indeed a small island (*isleta*) before the sand bar built up sufficiently to form an isthmus linking it with the rest of Gran Canaria. Unfortunately, the enticing heights of La Isleta, with their apparently un-matched views of the city, can no longer be approached, as they have been taken over by the military. Columbus landed at La Isleta during an early stage of his second voyage to America, in 1493.

As may be expected, La Isleta is well supplied with *tapas* bars, but tourists are recommended to be careful at night, as muggings have been reported in the quieter streets. Neverthe-less, no-one should miss the opportunity of following Calle de Luján Pérez, the second street northward from Calle La Naval to Bar Jamón (not Sunday evening or Monday, when it shuts), famous for the high quality of its hams, which are suspended in mainland-Spain fashion from the ceiling. Wine selection is lim-ited but at give-away prices.

Castillo de La Luz

A return southward ends at Calle de Juan Rejón, and a left turn leads to the city's most ancient and picturesque foundation, Castillo de la Luz, set in its small park overlooking Muelle Pesquero, the fishing jetty. An external plaque explains that the present fortress is seventeenth-century work, but this only refers to extensions made to the earlier tower of 1494, which is why a medieval appearance still prevails. The fort, the first to be built by the Spanish in the archipelago, occupies a strategic position,

As Chrismas approaches even the sand sculptures at Las Canteras adopt festive themes

*Although partly rebuilt in the seventeenth century,
Castillo de la Luz retains its medieval appearance*

and was, for much of its history, the only defensive tower protecting the approaches to the then tiny settlement of Las Palmas, which lay well to the south. Its main purpose, was to deter pirates. Alonso Fajaro, governor of Las Palmas in 1494, is believed to have been responsible for commissioning the original square tower, the flat roof of which served as a platform for cannon. Some allege, however, that a simple fortification had been constructed on the same site even earlier by Juan Rejón, soon after his initial attempt to conquer the island in 1475, but there is no evidence of this. A succession of naval battles was fought by the Spanish in the harbour of Las Palmas throughout the second half of the sixteenth century, all potential invaders, including Sir Francis Drake, being succesfully repulsed.

After years of neglect, during which the condition of the once isolated fort deteriorated, surrounding buildings were cleared and the small park was created around it; complete restoration of the structure took place in the late 1970s, and it now accommodates a theatre school. To the north of the fortress stretches the great port of Las Palmas.

Puerto de la Luz (Port of Light)

Where Puerto de la Luz has since been excavated there were formerly long beaches of sand. On one of these, the Spanish Conquistadores landed in 1478, as also, so it is believed, did Columbus, 14 years later. Development of Puerto de la Luz was sanctioned by the Spanish government in 1881 and, tactfully, a Telde engineer, León y Castillo, brother of Fernando, the Spanish Foreign Minister, was appointed to oversee the huge task: the family name is commemorated by the long thoroughfare that links the old city with the Santa Catalina district. Construction began in 1883, but was not completed until 1902, a tremendous amount of sand being removed. Extensions to the wharves have taken place at regular intervals, and the largest, Muelle Grande, officially renamed Muelle Reina Sofía, is now almost 2½ miles long.

Until the 1970s, when it became cheaper to travel from northern Europe to the Canaries by air rather than by sea, virtually all visitors to Gran Canaria arrived by ocean liner, and the decade 1960-70 was the busiest that the port has ever known. After this, container ships and immense tankers bacame the prime users of Puerto de la Luz, few holidaymakers disembarking. In recent years, however, pleasure cruising has made a comeback, and Las Palmas, strategically placed, is a popular calling point, particularly on route to the Caribbean. Columbus, no doubt, would have applauded this turn of events.

The South Korean fleet has been based here for many years, and the presence of a vast number of Russian sailors in Las Palmas is confirmed by the many signs in Russian to be seen in the shops and bars at the approaches to the port. Returning in the direction of Las Canteras, the Mercado del Puerto is sited where the coast road bends to the left. Basically a food market, it was entirely reconstructed in 1995. The Sunday morning flea market of Las Palmas, El Rastro, has been relocated in recent years from the Vegueta quarter, and is now held in front of it, overlooking the water.

Calle Albareda faces the market, continuing southward before diving underneath Parque de Santa Catalina. It is a road of scant interest to holidaymakers but, at number 55, within a small shopping arcade known as Soler de España, Indio is a rare example in the Canaries of an Indian restaurant. It serves a two-course set meal Monday to Friday (vegetarian on Mondays), and is authentic and very cheap — there is a take away service.

Playa de las Canteras — Southern Section
A succession of short streets link Calle Albareda with Las Canteras Beach, and most will wish to follow one of them in order to return to the promenade. Relatively few high-rise buildings overlook Las Canteras: most that do are hotels, some of which have been closed for years, indicative of mass tourism's preference for the sunnier beaches of the south; no doubt they will eventually be replaced by apartments for affluent residents. Nevertheless, aided by the splendid new promenade, the *paseo* successfully manages to escape seediness. Two very grand hotels overlook the beach, both five-star graded: Meliá las Palmas and Reina Isabel. Between them runs what is by far the most architecturally attractive stretch of the *paseo* , a mix of traditional Canary-style houses with pine balconies, and examples of Spanish Modernism — built in the 1920s on virgin sand. Behind lies

an ever-widening spit of land, laid out in the twentieth century to a grid pattern, the buildings here initially accommodated those connected with the new port, and later with tourism. There are few plazas or large shops, and virtually nothing of great architectural appeal has been built, but some of the city's finest hotels and restaurants are to be found in this western sector of Santa Catalina.

Almost half way along the Paseo de Las Canteras, at number 23, ice-cream lovers are recommended to sample at least one of the fifty home-made varieties at Heladería Atlántida; all are delicious and at a surprisingly modest price. At this point most eyes will be cast perpetually seaward to the undulating mountains and, at last, as the bay widens out, to the open sea. On reasonably clear days, Tenerife's great Mount Teide can be seen dominating the horizon, but to its left is another, but much nearer, extinct volcanic cone, with which it is sometimes confused. This is Montaña de Gáldar, which can be visited during an excursion to Gran Canaria's north coast (see page 141).

It is the changing light and cloud formations, as much as the golden sand and scenery, that make Las Canteras so special — even on cloudy days. In the morning, when the sun catches the mountains, the modelling is pronounced, and they appear to be quite close. Conversely, in the evening, with the setting sun behind them, they form a mysterious black silhouette, seemingly far distant.

It is hard to drag oneself away from the *paseo*, but a convenient point is where the Donosti bar is reached. Its location, on the corner with Calle Nicolás Estévanez, virtually coincides with the end of the rocks of La Barra, out to sea. Donosti has one of the widest ranges of *tapas* of any bar in Las Palmas and is extremely popular. It is only a few minutes' stroll from here to the great shops of Avenida de Mesa y López. Pass one block of Calle Nicolás Estévanez southward and turn first right.

Calle Doctor Grau Bassas leads to **Plazoleta de Faray**, a tiny square of great character, rare in modern Las Palmas. An important thoroughfare, Calle Fernando Guanarteme, runs diagonally north-eastward from this square, and after two blocks have been passed, a typical Las Palmas *churrosería*, at number 23, occupies the corner, right, with Calle Bernado de la Torre. At its southern end, the latter street bears right into **Plaza de España** (formerly Plaza de la Victoria), a popular late-evening assembly point for the city's youngsters, who frequent its outdoor cafés.

The Alcaravaneras Quarter & the Great Stores

Avenida de Mesa y López, which runs eastward from Plaza de España, is the most important shopping street in modern Las Palmas — chic boutiques vying with large department stores for the shopper's attention. At the first shop on the north side, fashion-conscious women can admire the latest creations of Spanish designer Adolfo Domínguez.

Before continuing further seaward, follow Calle Galicia, first right, to the Mercado Central of Las Palmas, where the usual lively stalls drastically undercut the prices demanded in the food halls of El Corte Inglés, just three blocks away. Overlooking the southern end of the market, at 5 Calle de Barcelona, is La Habana, open daily from 5am, and where the city's favourite *churros con chocolate* is served: the chocolate is so rich and thick that a spoon almost stands up in it.

Calle Valencia runs southward from the east side of the market and, seven blocks away, on its corner with Calle Manuel González Martín (number 36), Hermanos Rogelio, a popular bar/restaurant, serves genuine Canarian dishes Monday to Saturday at reasonable prices. Eat at the bar or at a table; there is always a lively atmosphere, which can become frenetic on big match days at the nearby football stadium, Estadio Insular.

On the northern side of the market, but not part of it, La Garriga, in Calle Néstor de la Torre, is renowned for its *charcuterie*, much of it ready prepared for an al fresco lunch.

Returning to Avenida de Mesa y López, few will be able to resist the welcoming entrance, at number 18, of the largest store in the Canaries, El Corte Inglés. This is a member of the chain of department stores now represented in most large Spanish cities, which has gained an international reputation. The quality of goods sold matches that of London's Selfridges, although the food halls are even more extensive. The name El Corte Inglés (The English Cut) surprises many. It has been inherited from the original tailor's shop in Madrid, where both the cloth imported and the styles followed were English. Don Ramón Areces borrowed £800 to buy the shop in 1934; it prospered, enabling him to build a department store empire with a turnover now approaching £3 billion. Cash was paid for each new store as it was built, and the group remained in private hands. When Areces died in 1989, he was believed to be the wealthiest man in Europe.

Although prices are not cheap, the quality is guaranteed, any faulty goods being replaced without question. Of particular interest to holidaymakers will be the usual electronics goods, wines and spirits and the food halls. In the latter will be found high quality *charcuterie* and cheeses from all over Spain — not just the Canary Islands. Look for the blue-veined goats milk cheese, *Cabrales*, from Asturias, not easily found elsewhere in Gran Canaria.

Almost directly opposite El Corte Inglés, at number 15, is Galerías Preciados, a member of rival department store chain, but not quite so up-market as El Corte Inglés.

 At the end of the busy avenue is a jetty with, at its southern end, the Club Náutico. This overlooks the golden sands of **Playa de las Alcaravaneras**, once popular, but since the busy Avenida Marítima del Norte was laid out directly behind it, the beach has become the haunt, almost exclusively, of local youngsters.

The Ciudad Jardín Quarter & Parque Doramas

Constructed in the 1930s, between the Alcaravaneras district and the commercial quarter of Lugo, Ciudad Jardín (Garden City) was inspired by English examples of the period, but with houses designed in a modern rationalist, rather than a traditional style. The area is pleasant, although lacking exceptional interest for tourists; its most attractive sector is sandwiched between Calle Pio XII and Calle León y Castillo, in the centre of which stands the **English Church**, entered from Calle Brasil. Walkers must be prepared to make several east or west deviations in order to maintain a southerly route towards Parque Doramas, as thoroughfares tend to be short and rarely interconnect directly ahead. Most, however, will prefer to take bus number 1 from Avenida de Mesa y López direct to Parque Doramas. Facing the park, the new bars/restaurants built around the jetty have become fashionable in the evenings.

Parque Doramas

Parque Doramas, the jewel of the Ciudad Jardín development, is the largest park in Las Palmas, and provides a green break immediately before the rather grey commercial quarter of Lugo is reached. To the right of its entrance is Hespeira, long regarded as the best florists in Las Palmas.

In the centre of the park, the Santa Catalina Hotel welcomes visitors to its bars, garden and restaurants. Opened in 1884, this five-star hotel is still the most prestigious in the city, the old-world atmosphere being unmatched elsewhere in the Canaries. Originally designed by McLauren, a Scottish architect, the hotel was also built by a British contractor. The Santa Catalina now incorporates a casino, where smart (but not formal) dress and a passport are required. *Tartana*, horsedrawn carriages may be hired outside the hotel for city tours.

To the south of the hotel, the **Pueblo Canario** (Canary Village) was designed by the painter Néstor de la Torre, who died suddenly in 1938, before it was finished. His brother Miguel, an architect, completed the building work, and then remodelled and extended the Santa Catalina Hotel. On Thursday evenings and Sunday mornings, Canary folk-dancing is performed in the Pueblo's courtyard, a rare opportunity for photographers, as traditional costumes are now seldom worn elsewhere on the island.

The **Museo Néstor** is to be found on the south side of the courtyard. Many of the artist's possesions are displayed, as also are his designs for several buildings in the *pueblo*, two of which were built, and a *parador* at Cruz de Tejeda, which was not. The most important of Néstor's works, however, are his set of eight paintings, *Poema de la Mer* (Poem of the Sea), displayed in a circular, domed gallery.

In the south-west corner of the park is a small **zoo**, and in the north-west corner, the Julio Navarro open-air swimming pool, only used in summer. Although the park ends at Calle Emilio Ley, gardens are laid out ahead, and reach up to the heights of Altavista. This quarter begins on the west side of Paseo de Chil, where there is a waterfall monument to Fernando León y Castillo.

Bus 3 departs from Triana's Avenida 1^0 de Mayo, linking the western hillside suburbs of Las Palmas before descending, via Avenida de Jose Mesa y López, to Parque de Santa Catalina and the port. For much of the journey, passengers gain splendid birds-eye views of the city.

Additional Information for Las Palmas

Accommodation

*Meliá las Palmas Hotel * * * * **
6 Calle Gomera
☎ 267600

*Santa Catalina Hotel * * * * **
Parque Doramas
☎ 243040

*Sandra P * **
Calle La Naval 9
☎ 262800

Eating Out

A'Vieira
26 Calle Sargento Llagas
☎ 27 99 56
Open daily 12 noon 4pm and 8pm-1am
(Galician cuisine)

House of Ming
30 Paseo de las Canteras
☎ 27 45 63
Open daily 12 noon-12 midnight
(Chinese)

Montesdeoca
10 Calle Montes de Oca
☎ 33 34 66
Open 12 noon-4pm and 8pm-12 midnight (not Sunday)
(Canary cuisine)

Places to Visit

Casa Museo de Colón
1 Calle Colón
Open 9am-6pm (not Saturday or Sunday)

Catedral de Santa Ana & Museo de Arte Sacro
20 Calle Espiritu Santo
Open Monday-Friday 9am-1.30pm and 4-6.30pm; Saturday 9am-2pm

Museo Canario
25 Calle Dr Chil
Open Monday-Friday 10am-1pm and 4-7.30pm

Pueblo Canario & Museo Néstor
Parque Doramas
Open Monday, Tuesday, Thursday, Friday 10am-1pm, 4-7pm; Saturday 10am-12 noon; Sunday 10.30am-1.30pm. Folk dancing Thursday 5.30-7pm; Sunday 11.30am-1pm. NB The Pueblo Canario is closed Wednesday

Tourist Information Office
Parque de Santa Catalina
☎ 26 46 23
Open Monday-Friday 9am-2pm

Itineraries From Las Palmas

5

Although the northern itineraries are all described from Las Palmas, motorists driving from the south who possess a good road map (and a degree of extra-sensory perception) will be able, in some cases, to avoid the city centre. Drivers should be aware that if they approach the city from the south and wish to take the 811 to Vega de San Mateo or the 813/817 to Teror then they **must not** miss the turn offs. Apart from an exit to the suburb of San José to the south of the city centre, these are the only two ways of leaving the *Autopista*; they are poorly signed, and if missed motorists will end up at the port or on the north coast. Those relying on the bus services run by Utinsa, must remember that all journeys begin and end at the Estación de Guagas in Las Palmas. As this is also where the Salcai buses between the southern resorts and Las Palmas deposit their passengers, connections may be made without difficulty. All the excursions already described from the south can also, of course, be started at Las Palmas. Those travelling by bus to Las Palmas from the south coast resorts should ensure that they take the 31, which departs every 30 minutes from Puerto Rico, following the *carretera*, and bypassing Playa del Inglés with its many stops, thereby reducing the journey time significantly.

The North Coast

Bañaderos • Cenobio de Valerón • San Felipe • Guía • Gáldar • Sardina del Norte • Cuevas de las Cruces • Hoya de Pineda • Agaete • Puerto de la Nieves • Agaete Valley/Los Berrazales

Gran Canaria's north coast, well-watered and fertile, was a popular residential area of the Guanches, and all its existing townships of any size were established long before the Spanish conquest. Like most of the west coast, its appeal consists of dramatic cliffs and strange-shaped rocks, rather than glorious sandy beaches. It is important to select good weather for this excursion if possible: most of the coast frequently tends to be affected by the cloud that builds up over the central mountains and can turn showery.

As opposed to the west side of the island, a good road closely follows the north coast, and bus services are frequent, particularly between Las Palmas and Gáldar. The approach to the north coast road from Las Palmas is made via its dreary south-west suburb of Guanarteme. Sad to reflect that delightful, Maspalomas-style sand dunes at the back of Playa de Las Canteras were removed in the 1950s for its construction.

If staying in the Las Canteras area, particularly at the south end, some may prefer to walk or taxi as far as the bridge that crosses the *barranco* after Guanarteme has been left. Here, the north coast buses stop, thus obviating the slow and lengthy journey to the bus station at Parque San Telmo and back again.

Buses 101, 102, 103 and 105 all follow the same coastal roads to Gáldar; the 101, a very limited service, continues to San Nicolás de Tolentino (see page 72), via Agaete; the 103 links Agaete with the coast at Puerto de las Nieves, and the 102 continues along the valley from Agaete to Los Berrazales.

Overlooking the sea, and serving as an introduction to the grand coastal scenery, the Atlantes Monument takes the form of an 8m (26ft) high figure of volcanic rock. This was sculpted by a Canario, Tony Gallardos, as a tribute to the Atlantic Ocean.

Bañaderos & Puente de Silva

There are fine views of the receding Las Canteras beach and La Isleta from the road as it curves northward. At the small town of Bañaderos, a left turn branches inland to Arucas and Teror; some may prefer to make the detour at this stage, and it is described on pages 147-152. Bañaderos, with a maritime esplanade, is named from its natural rock pools, in one of which a Guanche princess was captured by Spanish invaders.

Several steep *barrancos* reach the sea after Pagador has been passed; two of them are crossed by the Puente de Silva, a double-stage viaduct, the highest in Spain, and known locally as the Salto del Canario (Canario's Leap).

It is here that the great banana plantations of the north begin. Unfortunately for the Canarios, cheaper bananas are now obtainable from elsewhere to supply the European market, and the crop is in decline, much of it now unattended and growing wild. This does, however, provide the attractive, but once rare, sight of bright yellow bananas hanging from the trees; formerly, all were picked in their unripe green state for slow ripening in the holds of ships and warehouses.

Cenobio de Valerón & San Filipe

The next left turn off the 810, at Barrio de la Atalaya, leads to Cenobio de Valerón, the only Guanche site of importance in Gran Canaria currently open to visitors.

Overlooking the *barranco*, on the south side of the road, a great archway in the cliff may be approached via a flight of steps. This marks the entrance to the *cenobio*, a pagan version of a nunnery, in which lived Harimaguadas: virtuous ladies who had been selected from good families for a life devoted to religion and the praise of the god, Alcorac. In spite of their celibacy, it was the

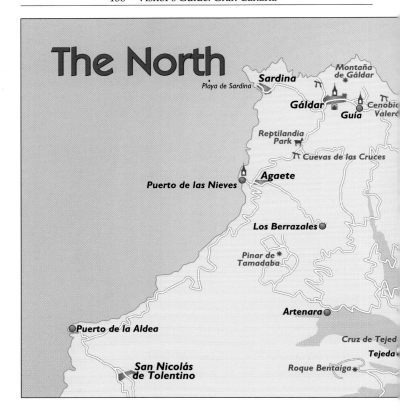

Harimaguadas whose duty it was to prepare 15-year old daughters of the Guanche nobility for marriage. As part of this task, they fed the girls fattening dishes, as it was believed that only women with wide hips and full breasts would produce healthy children.

Incorporated in the complex are approximately a hundred small cells; there is evidence that each was fitted with a wooden cover, and presumably the cells were used for storage. Guanche artefacts have been discovered here but none remain in situ.

A Tagoror meeting place above the cave is indicated by the circle of stones.

By tradition, it was down the face of this mountain that an early but unsuccesful Spanish invader, Diego da Silva, and his party of men were led on route to their vessels, where all were released and directed homewards. It would appear that the Guanches hoped their magnanimity would be rewarded by an end to European invasions; they were wrong, and the Cenobio de Valerón later served as a Guanche hideout during the final and succesful Spanish assault on their island.

The same road continues eastward, passing beneath the 810, to the fishing village of **San Felipe**, with its pebbly beach. As at Bañaderos, there are natural swimming pools in the flat rocks.

✳ However, of greater interest at San Felipe is El Roque, a St Michael's Mount in miniature, but with fishermen's houses grouped around narrow lanes on the the rock itself rather than below it.

A return to the main road and a westward continuation along it soon brings visitors to the town of Santa María de Guía de Gran Canaria, or simply Guía, as it is usually called. From the town centre, those without a car may hire a taxi to Cenobio de Valerón and San Felipe's beach, should time permit

Guía

Guía is a prosperous agricultural town, which now virtually merges Gáldar, with its slightly larger neighbour. It was the birthplace of the most famous Canarian sculptor, José Luján Pérez (1756-1815), whose work is seen in the cathedral at Las Palmas; further examples are to be found in Guía's church of Santa María, founded in 1491. A mass pilgrimage to the church, known as the Romería de las Marías, is made during the last week in September on a variable date. Traditional costumes are worn and there is much dancing and feasting to end this popular event.

✳ Just outside Guía, at 17 Carretera General Lomo Guillen, on the main road to Gáldar, is the Artesanía Canaria, better known as Arturo's Bar, where the famous local cheese, *queso de flora*, may be eaten or purchased to take away. This cheese is made from goats' milk flavoured with the blossoms of a type of thistle known as cardoon. Arturo serves it with the surprising combination of garlic potatoes and hot toast. A selection of Canary wines, difficult to find elsewhere, may also be tasted: the dry, red Monte Déniz, from the Santa Brígida region, is the best accompaniment to *queso de flora*, but those with a sweet tooth should ask for the white Vino de Licor Dulce, which is probably similar to the Canary malmsey wine *malvasías*, so popular in Shakespeare's England. Crafts as well as cheeses may be purchased here; particularly attractive are the knives with inlaid bone handles, known as *cachillos*, and *cajas*-decorated boxes, both locally made.

Buses, of course, link Guía with Gáldar, but the distance between the towns is short, and many without cars will opt to walk, particularly as the 810 has lost its dual carriageway status at Guía, and there are attractive views from the road along the Barranco de Gáldar,which opens up to join the lush Agaete valley.

As Gáldar is approached, the 'mini Mount Teide', distantly observed from Playa de Las Canteras, comes into view to the north. Known as the Montaña or Pico de Gáldar, this extinct volcano retains a symmetrical, conical shape, but its stony slopes have led to its being referred to, rather unkindly, as 'the slag heap'.

Gáldar

In addition to being an agricultural town, Gáldar is the commercial centre of Gran Canaria's north west. A market is held every Thursday morning in Plaza Mayor, but cheap clothing now dominates, and it is not very exciting.

Gáldar was a regional capital of the Guanches, possibly one of the earliest in Gran Canaria, and artefacts made by them and discovered locally are displayed in a small museum in the town hall; this faces the church from the west side of the plaza, where there grows a venerable dragon tree, of which the locals are rather proud.

Gáldar's church is dedicated to **Santiago** (St James) **de los Caballeros**, as the town fell to the Spanish on 25 July, St James's Feast Day. An early seventeenth-century church, built where the Guanche king's house and a small Spanish fort once stood, was rebuilt and enlarged in the eighteenth century. Within are sculptures by Pérez, and the *pilar verde* (green font) in which, by tradition, Guanche converts to Christianity were baptized.

Antonio Padrón (1920-68), a Gáldar artist, followed the Impressionist style, and his work is exhibited in the house where he painted, **Casa-Museo de Antonio Padrón**, at 1 Calle Drago, and where, apart from 5 years studying in Madrid, he spent his entire life.

From the north side of Plaza Mayor, a narrow street leads through banana plantations towards the coast where, approximately 1 mile distant, **La Guancha**, an ancient necropolis, was discovered in 1935. Truncated rock circles, right of the path, are the burial sepulchres of Guanches.

The extinct volcano of Pico de Gáldar overlooks the town of Gáldar

The grey-sand beach of Sardina del Norte, backed by volcanic cliffs

Discovered in the nineteenth century, Gáldar's most famous attraction, the **Cueva Pintada**, contains the only Guanche wall paintings yet found in the Canaries. Almost square in plan, the cave's 3m (10ft) high walls are decorated with geometric paintings in red, white and black. Experts believe that the work was executed around the time of the birth of Christ, but its significance is a mystery; the apparent rarity of such decoration may indicate that an important Guanche chief inhabited the cave. In 1970, deterioration of the paintings had become apparent and the cave was blocked up pending restoration. Check whether it has reopened before visiting. There is a reproduction of the cave at the Museo Canario in Las Palmas (see page 120).

Sardina del Norte

A local bus to and from Sardina follows the second turn right (140) off the main road, once Gáldar has been left, for 6km (4 miles). Many will find the beach and cafés of the small port the most attractive on the north coast, even though the sand is the usual grey colour. The coastal scenery is magnificent, with particularly good views from Punta de Sardina, a headland to the north, which embrace Tenerife in clear weather. Sardina has a small church and, at the end of its sheltered bay, a lighthouse.

Reptilandia Park

Motorists returning towards the 810 will be able to follow a track, right, to Reptilandia Park. Others must take the Gáldar/Agaete bus (101, 102, 103) from the main road, and alight at the Cruz de Pineda stop. A large sign near this indicates the track to Reptilandia Park, which spreads over the lower slopes of another stony, extinct volcano, Montaña Almago. The most exotic specimens of reptiles in the collection of over a hundred species are the poisonous snakes and frogs, all of which are kept safely behind glass in the visitors centre. However, the bulk of the reptiles on view are harmless lizards, some of them brightly coloured, which are kept in open enclosures.

Cuevas de las Cruces & Hoya de Pineda

A minor road leads eastward from the Cruz de Pineda bus stop to the Cuevas de las Cruces, a short walk away. These caves are still occupied, many of them having been in the possesion of the same family for generations, although it is almost certain that the original residents were Guanches. Nearby, the **Ermita de San Isidro el Viejo** is one of the tiniest chapels on the island.

Although most will now prefer to make directly for Agaete, on the 810, an infrequent bus from Gáldar continues to Hoya de Pineda, renowned for its home-made pottery, and then follows the Barranco de Gáldar southward, a most attractive route. To the east rises Montaña Vergara where, until the eighteenth century, branches of pine trees were cut for the pagan Bajada de la Rama rite at Agaete (see below). The bus continues to Valleseco, from where another bus, the 21, departs for Teror and Las Palmas.

Agaete

Standing at the entrance to the Barranco de Agaete, the most fertile valley in the north of the island, the town's main purpose, as might be expected, is to serve as a distribution centre for agricultural produce. Whitewashed 'cubic' houses give Agaete a very Moorish appearance.

On 4 August each year the town is witness to the only Guanche rite still performed anywhere in the Canaries. Known as Bajada de la Rama (Cutting of the Branch), local residents treck to the Tamadaba pine forest at dawn, returning to Agaete with huge branches that they have cut from the trees — a 6 to 8 hour expedition. The branches are then taken to Puerto de las Nieves, nearby, where the sea is symbolically beaten with them. Originally, the purpose of this superstitious rite was to persuade the autumn rains not to fail, but it is now just an excuse for a *fiesta*, and has long been Christianized. No longer does the rite end at the shore, as, after it has ended, the townfolk gather in Agaete, singing and dancing in the streets until the early hours of the following morning.

Both the 101 and the much more frequent 103 buses link Agaete with Puerto de las Nieves, via a minor road, but it is not a long walk.

Puerto de las Nieves

Many surmise, erroneously, that Nieves (Snows) refers to the gleaming winter snows of Mount Teide, which can usually be seen clearly from here, but it is, in fact, a painting in the **Ermita de las Nieves** chapel that gave the small port its name. This sixtenth-century Flemish triptych, generally regarded as the greatest artistic treasure of Gran Canaria, was brought to the island by an Italian, Antón Cerezo, who settled on the island. Due to its subject matter, the work is known as the *Virgen de las Nieves* (Virgin of the Snows). Unfortunately, due to the painting's great value, the recently restored chapel is locked unless Mass is being celebrated; Sunday, therefore, is the best day to make a visit. If the chapel is open, also look out for the model sailing ships on display.

Puerto de las Nieves, primarily a fishing village, possesses two beaches, both of stone and dark sand: foaming breakers often make swimming impossible. To the south, the jagged peaks of the Tamadaba massif provide a dramatic backdrop. A smart new promenade, Paseo de las Poetas (Poet's Walk), has made access between the beaches much easier.

Sternly pointing skyward, a slim volcanic rock, known as Dedo de Dios (Finger of God), is located at the south end of the beach. From a distance, the rock can be difficult to identify because, particularly on dull days, it merges into the background of equally black cliffs.

From Agaete, the 102 bus follows the delightful, 7km (4½ miles) long, Barranco de Agaete to its head at Los Berrazales. Some buses pick up at Puerto de las Nieves on route to Las Palmas, but not, unfortunately, in the other direction, on route to Los Berrazales.

Agaete Valley/Los Berrazales

As has been said, the Agaete valley is where much of Gran Canaria's exotic fruit, such as figs, papayas, mangoes and avocados, is grown. Mountain streams and the narrowness of the valley create a constantly mild, humid climate, which is ideal for plantlife: nowhere else on the island are wild flowers seen in such profusion.

Curative spring water at Berrazales is bottled locally, but there are no longer public baths for sufferers from rheumatism.

Bus 102 returns to Las Palmas via Agaete, where a change

The Dedo de Dios (Finger of God) at Puerto de las Nieves
may be difficult to identify unless the light is just right

must be made to the 101 by those continuing southward to San Nicolás de Tolentino (page 72) and thence Puerto de Mogán. Although nothing exceptional is passed on route to San Nicolás, some invigorating coastal scenery can be glimpsed; passengers should try to find a seat on the right-hand side of the bus.

Motorists returning to Las Palmas may have sufficient time to make a detour to Arucas and Teror by turning right at Bañaderos, following the 813. Bus 215, which starts on the coast at Pagador, also connects these towns, via Bañaderos, Cardones, Tenoya and Tamaraceite.

A roadside church at El Palmital west of Moya

The Picturesque Northern Towns & Tamadaba Pine Forest

Arucas • Firgas • Moya • Teror • Artenara • Tamadaba • Acusa

From Las Palmas, motorists will take the 813 to Arucas; this runs inland and then keeps parallel with the north-coast road; buses 205, 206, 209, 211 and 234 link Las Palmas with Arucas, following various routes.

Arucas

Arucas is still given the accolade as the third largest town in Gran Canaria (after Las Palmas and Telde), even though the conurbation based on Playa del Inglés is now very much more extensive.

Rum lovers may already have tasted the pale gold liquid in bottles displaying the name Ron Arucas, which will be found in all bars in Gran Canaria. This rum has been made in Arucas virtually ever since sugar cane was introduced to the islands, and is the prime reason why the crop is still grown in the area. The Ron Arehucas (the old spelling of Arucas) distillery is located surprisingly close to the town centre, and visitors are welcomed with a tipple. Not to be missed in Arucas are the town's subtropical public gardens.

Architecturally, Arucas is dominated by its huge church of **San Juan Bautista** (St John the Baptist). Consecrated in 1917, local craftsmen laboured on the Neo-Gothic building for almost a century. A contrast between white-painted plaster and exposed basalt, in the traditional Canary style, enlivens the façade. Within are found works by local artist, Juan de Miranda, a sixteenth-century Flemish painting of the Nativity and, of greatest importance, a carved figure of Christ, by Manuel Ramos. Also noteworthy is the stained glass, rated the best in Gran Canaria. Locals, with an excess of local pride, often refer to their church, erroneously, as the 'cathedral'. From the town centre, a short minor road climbs northward to the summit of ☐ Montaña de Arucas, from where the coastal views towards La Isleta are outstanding.

Firgas & Moya

From Arucas, the 814 runs westward to Firgas, a name with

which visitors to Gran Canaria soon become familiar, as the eponymous best-selling mineral water on the island is produced from the natural springs which flow south of the village. Moya is reached by making a brief return northward on the 814, followed by a left turn on the 100, and another on the 160. The 211 bus from Arucas follows the same route; buses 116 and 117 link Moya directly with Las Palmas.

Doramas, the last Guanche king, had his military headquarters at Moya, and the town was also the birthplace, at 1 Paseo Tomás Morales, of the poet Tomás Morales (1885-1921), whose house may be visited.

Of greatest interest in Moya is the location of its twin-towered church, **Nuestra Señora de la Candelaria**, perched dramatically on the cliff overlooking the Moya *barranco*. Its position is best appreciated from across the *barranco* on the 150 to Guía, rather from the town itself. Earlier churches on this site, dating from the sixteenth century, were apparently unable to survive the exposed situation, wind and rain gradually eroding their structures.

The 150 from Moya ascends its *barranco* and, after 3km (2 miles), a minor road branches off to **Los Tilos**, the last significant forest of laurel trees in Gran Canaria. Formerly, laurel forests almost covered the north of the island: this example is now protected.

No roads link Moya directly with Teror and, as has been said, a return must be made to Firgas before proceeding, on the 814, to Gran Canaria's most picturesque town. Those who have opted to continue directly southward to Teror from Arucas will have taken the 230, which is also followed by the 215 bus. On route, it is possible to visit the grounds of the Aula de la Naturaleza, a nature study centre, at **Osorio**, which occupies an early twentieth-century house, built in English colonial style. As at Los Tilos, the forest here is of laurel, although it is much smaller in extent.

Those following the 814 by car or bus from Firgas will pass the bottling plant (Aguas de Firgas) of the mineral water, which is available in aerated (*gas*) or non-aerated (*sin gas*) form. The road then takes an abrupt turn eastward, descending in sharp bends to Teror, lying serenely in the valley below.

Teror is noted for its attractive pine balconies

The galleried patio of Casa Museo Patronas de la Virgen in Teror

Teror

Holidaymakers in Gran Canaria should make every effort to visit this beautiful town, which bus 216 links directly with Las Palmas. Here will be seen the finest examples on the island of pine balconies, the hallmark of Canary architecture.

The most picturesque quarter of Teror is centred on its church, **Nuestra Señora del Pino**. Its name refers to the tradition that, in 1481, the Virgin Mary appeared on the branch of a pine tree to the village priest. The church, founded in 1515 as a simple building without aisles, was gradually extended. In 1718, fireworks for a local *fiesta*, stored in the sacristy, accidentally exploded, causing extensive damage. As rebuilding of the church depended on local finance, and it was not until the end of the eighteenth century that the new building was completed. A baroque façade, as usual, combines white paintwork with exposed stone. Separate from the main church is the octagonal bell tower, which is surprisingly designed to imitate the late Gothic, sixteenth-century Manueline style of Portugal.

Within, the ceiling is coffered and there is some fine carving. Set in the reredos of the high altar, an illuminated alabaster Madonna and Child carving, known as the Virgin of the Pines, is sumptuously robed. This was made in 1767, and the throne of solid silver, the work of a Tenerife silversmith, is believed to be contemporary with it. The Blessed Virgin of Teror is the patron saint of Gran Canaria, and there are great celebrations on her feast day, 8 September, when pilgrims arrive in decorated carts.

Until the present century, it was a superstitious custom, whenever drought or a locust plague threatened, to march in procession from Teror to Las Palmas cathedral, bearing this figure, which was supplicated to intervene. Even today, the carving is accredited with healing powers. From the eighteenth century, gifts of precious stones were presented to the Virgin, but in 1975 burglars broke in through the roof of the church and stole the most precious gems.

Located on the same square is the ancient **Casa de la Villa** (town hall), and its patio may be entered.

The street that directly faces the church is renowned for its balconies. Canary balconies are often canopied and usually face north, emphasizing that they are certainly not intended for sunbathing.

Immediately left is the **Casa Museo Patronas de la Virgen**, a mansion with a galleried patio, which has been in the ownership of the aristocratic Manrique de la Lara family since the seventeenth century, and where its members frequently continue to reside in the summer (Teror is a popular inlandsummer resort). For the rest of the year, apart from Fridays, the house is open to the public, and the family's collection of furniture and objets d'art may be viewed.

The name of Teror's Plaza de Bolivar commemorates the birth in a house overlooking this square of the mother of Simón Bolivar, who gained independence from the Spanish for several colonies in South America, one of which, Bolivia, bears his name.

Every Sunday morning, the market held in the town is particularly renowned for local produce. Always available in Teror is nougat (*turrón*) and intricate lacework made by nuns in the nearby convent. A local *charcuterie* store, Las Nueces, is renowned for the quality of its home-made *chorizo* and black pudding.

Good food can be obtained from Bar Americano, facing the church, and Bar Diego, in Calle de General Franco, where the *carne de cabra* (goat meat) is delicious. For those requiring a more formal meal, El Secuestro offers local specialities and charcoal grilled meat (closed Mondays).

From Teror, the 814 leads directly to San Mateo (or Vega de San Mateo) passing close to the extinct volcano of **Pino Santo**, where the miracle of the virgin's appearance is said to have occurred. Here can be seen the only dragon tree growing wild in the north of Gran Canaria.

San Mateo is described on page 158. From Teror westward, the 814 links with the 110, which climbs steadily uphill towards Valleseco and the mountain village of Artenara. Bus 220 from Las Palmas follows the route.

On the left is passed the Balcón de Zamora *mirador*, on the summit of which is a large bar/restaurant specializing in Canary dishes. The road to Artenara passes through the villages of **Valleseco** and **Lanzarote**, the name of the latter, like that of the island of Lanzarote, commemorating Lancellotto Mallocello, the fourteenth-century Genoese navigator, who rediscovered the Canary Islands. Unattractive piles of volcanic rock, known as *malpais* (bad country), is gradually being hidden by the planting of pine trees.

Just after Cuevas Corcho, the 110 abruptly turns right and climbs steeply.It should be noted that both the left turn at this point and that which follows lead to the Cruz de Tejeda and the high peaks of Gran Canaria (see pages 84-90). On route to Artenara there are tremendous views from **Pinos de Gáldar** to the north coast. The name of this viewpoint reflects that the cone-shaped Montaña de Gáldar can be seen in the distance.

Artenara & Pinar de Tamadaba

Artenara, at 1,219m (3,998ft) above sea level, is the highest village in Gran Canaria. Caves in the region, some still occupied, indicate that the Guanches lived in the area. There is a small church in the village, but of greater interest is the **Santuario de la**

Virgen de la Cuevita, the chapel of the patron saint of Artenara. It is reached by a winding road, which begins opposite the church. A cottage industry of replicating Guanche artefacts and red pottery for sale to tourists has evolved in the village. The famous La Silla restaurant at Artenara is located partly in a cave, partly on a terrace with superb views. It closes at sunset.

Continuing westward from Artenara, the 3.1 road encircles Pinar de Tamadaba, the largest forest of Canary pines on the island, where it ends abruptly at the entrance to a forestry station. The trees even cover the summit of the **Pico de Tamadaba** (1,444m, 4,736ft), which rises from its centre. Within the ICONA picnic site there is a welcome spring-water drinking fountain, and rocky ledges offer Gran Canaria's finest views of Mount Teide emerging from the sea.

The quickest return for motorists to Las Palmas is made via Cruz de Tejeda, following the 811 San Mateo/Santa Brígida road, a route which is described from the direction of Las Palmas in the next section. Those making for the southern resorts will follow the 811 from Cruz de Tejeda to Ayacata, followed by the 815 to San Bartolomé, and the 12.1, via Fataga, to Playa del Inglés, the route described (in reverse order) on pages 78-84.

An exciting alternative route, however, which passes a number of mountain reservoirs (*presas*) is to return in the direction of Artenara, but branch off on the 3.4, the second turning right, in the direction of San Nicolás via the village of Acusa, which is signposted. It must be said, however, that those who suffer from vertigo are not advised to make the journey, as hairpin bends and unprotected sheer drops from the mountain ledge that the road follows are numerous.

Drivers should bear in mind that there is no filling station until San Nicolás, 48km (30 miles) from Artenara, is reached. **Acusa**, merely a tiny church, an unused school and a handful of houses, stands on its *vega* (flat tableland), which is distinguished by cultivation in the midst of barren landscape.

On the right is the **Presa de Calendario**, the first of four

opposite: Houses nestle in the huge crater of the extinct volcano at Bandama

reservoirs which will be passed; the next, also on the right, is the **Presa del Parralillo**, a mysterious looking stretch of water with a greenish hue, even though there is scant greenery to be reflected in it from the bare mountainsides. Some of the best views of this reservoir are to be gained from the old windmill overlooking it.

A descent on the 16.4 leads to the **Presa del Caldero de las Niñas** and, on the left, **Presa de Siberio**. The intrepid are permitted to walk on top of the wall of the latter's dam, but not to swim in it (so the notice says) — as if one would wish to!

The remainder of the journey to San Nicolás de Tolentino (page 72) is unremarkable; the road passes through the fertile Barranco de la Aldea, but its acres of cultivation are protected by unsightly, shimmering plastic.

The 'Paradise' Route to the Mountains

Jardín Canario • La Calzada • Tafira Alta & Monte Coella • La Atalaya • Caldera de Bandama • Santa Brígida • Vega de San Mateo
This relatively short excursion begins at the Carretera del Centro (the 811), which divides the Vegueta and Triana quarters of Las Palmas; it then runs above the Barranco de Guiniguada and ends at Vega de San Mateo. On Sunday mornings, an important market is held at San Mateo, and in order not to miss it some may wish to proceed directly to this small town. A continuation from San Mateo to the high mountains is easily made.

Numerous buses, all begining at Las Palmas, are routed along various stages of the 811. The 00 bus stops at the entrance to Jardín Canario and continues to Santa Brígida; the 58 and 59 terminate at Tafira Alta; the 301 and 302 terminate at Santa Brígida; the 303 and 305 continue to Vega de San Mateo and (the 305 only) to Cruz de Tejeda.

What are undoubtedly the most desirable residential suburbs of Las Palmas spread along the 811, the lush gardens of their houses, always green and blossoming, giving the impression of a large park studded with buildings. The entire area is renowned throughout the Canaries for the high quality of its restaurants, catering not only for wealthy Canarios, but also for the sizeable number of foreign immigrants residing in this part of the island, attracted by its benign climate.

Feathery eucalyptus trees, of Australian origin, line the road, while in the valleys below, spiky palm trees provide an exotic contrast. Surely, if paradise exists, it must look like this.

On route to Jardín Canario, the road winds up to the University Campus of Gran Canaria. Below lies **Tafira Baja**, Surprisingly, the Tirma (a Guanche cry of freedom) chocolate factory is located here, far from the west coast town of Tirma, where one might expect to find it. The quality of this chocolate is very good, even though it sells at much lower prices than imported brands: chocoholics should look out for it!

Jardín Canario

Lying just north of the 811, this immense garden, officially called the Viera y Clavijo Canary Garden, was founded by Sventenius, a Swede, and opened in 1952. The layout is informal, and a natural appearance has been achieved. As would be expected, most of the specimens are from the Canary Islands, but virtually any plantlife that will thrive in Gran Canaria's balmy climate is eligible for inclusion. Particularly impressive are the towering cacti from South Africa.

Overlooking the garden and the surrounding countryside from its cliff- top location is the Jardín Canario restaurant, formerly a residential *parador*. Canary specialities and the ususal international dishes are on offer (check if credit cards are accepted yet).

La Calzada

South of the garden spreads the village of La Calzada, where there are two restaurants worth seeking out: Grill La Raqueta, located on the *carretera*, specializing in charcoal grills, and Los Conejos, at 18 La Calzada (closed Tuesdays), where the rabbit, Canary-style, is superb.

At the end of the village, a bridge crosses the *barranco*. Two Spanish monks, bent on converting Guanches to Christianity, were murdered in caves that had been excavated in the cliff on the far side; they are now known as **Cuevas de los Frailes** (Caves of the Monks).

Tafira Alta & Monte Coello

A return to the 811 leads to Tafira Alta, possibly the most sought-after (and expensive) of all the residential areas in the north of the island. Only the extremely wealthy can afford to live here. It was developed at the turn of the century by the British, many of whom were making a fortune from their introduction of new crops to the Canaries, particularly bananas. The late-nineteenth-century Los Frailes Hotel, built by an Englishman, still functions in the town, on the *carretera*. Tafira Alta merges to the south with Monte Coello (or simply El Monte), the most important wine producing town in Gran Canaria.

From Monte Coello, the 13.5 leads eastward to Gran Canaria's most famous extinct volcanic crater, Caldera Bandama. Buses 311 or 312 provide a service to Bandama from Las Palmas, following the 811 before turning eastward on the 320 and then the 13.6 to La Atalaya.

La Atalaya

It is said that more than 1,000 Guanche caves exist in and around La Atalaya, many of them still inhabited. Pottery made locally can be purchased in the village.

Caldera Bandama

The 13.6 now winds northward tyo join the 13.5, spiralling round the slopes of **Pico de Bandama**, which rises 574m (1,883ft) above sea level. The fertile crater (*caldera*) has a circumference of about one kilometre, and a depth of 200m (650ft). Much of it is arable land and farm buildings below may clearly be seen from the crater's rim.

On the west side of the mountain is Spain's oldest golf course, the Club de Golf de Las Palmas, founded by British residents in 1891.

A return to the 811, either at Monte Coello or the 312 junction further south, must be made before continuing to the high mountains. The road climbs ever upward, and the scenery becomes even more idyllic as the dramatic background of peaks is approached. In late January/early February, when the almond

opposite: The fertile countryside near Vega de San Mateo

trees are in blossom, this part of Gran Canaria is quite breathtaking in its pastoral magnificence — if depicted on a chocolate box it would be considered unacceptably over the top.

Santa Brígida
Santa Brígida must be passed before the ribbon of luxury villas is interrupted by open country, but it will be noted that on both sides of the road buildings struggle heroically to retain a hold on precipitous mountain slopes. Santa Brígida is of no particular interest to tourists, in fact, it is hard to clearly distinguish architecturally between any of the fashionable developments along this mountain road. A famous Santa Brígida restaurant, La Grutas de Artiles, is located at Las Meleguinas, and offers beautifully prepared Spanish and international dishes. Two of the dining rooms are set in caves and, in summer, clients may use the private swimming pool.

Lovers of German food should visit Mano de Hierro, founded by German-born Karl Kenegeter, and now run by his son. Knowledgeable German visitors enthuse over the restaurant's home-made sausages and *patés*, which are now almost impossible to obtain made in the traditional style in their own country; the *quesadilla* (cheesecake) is exceptional.

Vega de San Mateo (San Mateo)
A drop in temperature often becomes apparent at Vega de San Mateo, due to its altitude. The small town is still chiefly dependant on agriculture, and retains a slightly more venerable appearance than its neighbours, although, like them, it is also a popular residential centre. On Sunday mornings, a large farmer's market is held, where the prices of the fruit and vegetables are said to be the lowest on the island; locally produced white cheese, *queso San Mateo*, is naturally found at its best here. Anyone wishing to purchase a goat will also find a bargain!

 In Avenida Tinamar, the **Casa-Museo de Chó Zacarías**, a converted farmhouse of rustic charm, displays a collection of early Canarian artefacts, furnishings and pottery. Incorporated is a *bodega* specializing in local wines, and, of course, *queso San Mateo*.

A restaurant, La Taberna de Chó Zacarías (closed Mondays),

serves Spanish regional dishes; at the time of writing credit cards are not accepted, but prices are most reasonable.

Near the museum, in the same street, El Secuestro II, also closed Mondays, is recommended for its charcoal grills. Two more San Mateo restaurants, both of which close Tuesdays, and are located on the Carretera del Centro are: La Vaguetilla, which offers a varied cuisine including barbecues, and Martell (at El Madronal), designed as a typical *bodega*, which stocks just about every cheese and variety of wine produced in Gran Canaria, in addition to Spanish regional dishes.

Virtually all holidaymakers who approach the high mountains from Las Palmas will take the route just described, as the Carretera del Centro is by far the easiest and fastest way of reaching them. Many, therefore, will continue ahead to Cruz de Tejeda, from San Mateo to the mountains (see pages 84-90).

Additional Information

Places To Visit

Gáldar
Museum
Town Hall

Casa-Museo de Antonio Padrón
1 Calle Drago

Moya
Casa Museo Tomás Morales
1 Paseo Tomás Morales
Open: Monday-Friday 3-5pm, Saturday and Sunday 10am-2pm

Tafira
Jardín Canario
Open daily, but closes 1-3pm.
Admission free.

Teror
Casa-Museo Patronas de la Virgen
Open: daily apart from Fridays and when the family is in residence in the sumer.

San Mateo
Casa-Museo de Chó Zacarías
Avenida Tinamar

Fact File

above: Only the large hotels boast heated swimming pools

Accommodation

Most holidaymakers will arrive in Gran Canaria with accommodation already booked as part of an inclusive package. Hotels in Gran Canaria are graded from one to five stars, *hostals* from one to three stars, and *pensiones* from one to two stars. Accommodation is grouped as follows: H — Hotel, HR — Residential Hotel (no dining room), HA — Hotel Apartments (or Apartotel), RA — Serviced Apartments (no dining room), P — *Pensiones*, little different from *hostals*, CV — Vacation Complex (hotel with sports facilities). Apartments are also graded — from one to three keys.

Those who are keen on swimming (or at least splashing about in water) are advised to obtain written confirmation that they will have access to a heated pool. For most of the year, only the hardiest will wish to bathe in the sea, due to the cold Canary current, and only in the summer is the sun strong enough to heat swimming pool water sufficiently without assistance.

Additional information, specific to individual resorts, is given throughout this book where applicable.

Those who have not already reserved accommodation will find that the tourist offices at Gando airport, Playa del Inglés or Las Palmas will be able to assist. Spanish National Tourist Offices can supply, on application before departure, lists of accommodation in Gran Canaria, including current tariffs (see page 182).

Arrival

Virtually all holidaymakers now fly to Gran Canaria, arriving at Gando Airport. There are frequently bargain-priced chartered flights and packages available for last minute bookings, particularly before and after the Christmas and Easter holiday periods. Baggage and immigration clearances are usually speedy, particularly for visitors from EU countries. Tour operators transport those who have booked accommodation with them to their hotels or apartments by coach.

Gando airport is approximately a 30-minute drive away from Las Palmas and 30 minutes from the southern resorts.

Visitors travelling independantly will find that a Salcai bus to Las Palmas operates 24 hours a day from directly outside the airport concourse. However, the vast majority, who wish to stay in the sunny south, are less fortunate — no bus whatsoever stops conveniently at the airport. There is a bus, but this involves scrambling across a dual carriage-way to its far side — not to be recommended. It is far safer to take the bus to the Las Palmas bus station and then come back again. Those not on a budget can, of course, pay the outrageous 3,500 pesetas set fare demanded by taxi drivers to conduct them from Gando to the Costa Canaria. Locals allege that this extraordinary situation prevails because the island's 'taxi mafia' has been able to persuade the authorities that an economically-priced bus service from the airport for holidaymakers would not be advantageous! It is easier to make the return journey to the airport from the south directly by bus but, once again, access to the concourse is not straightforward. An additional hazard is that some bus drivers seem to be involved in the alleged taxi drivers' racket, neglecting to stop at the airport, or driving on with the departed passenger's luggage still locked in their hold. Take care!

Gando airport is 22km (13½ miles) from Las Palmas and 30km (18½ miles) from Playa del Inglés; the telephone number is 25 41 40.

Banks & Money

Most banks are open Monday to Friday 9.30am-2pm (1pm Saturday), but specialist exchange organisations operate for most of the day. The banks' foreign exchange services can be extremely slow and pedantic, and a minimum standard charge of 600 pesetas is made for each transaction, however small the amount involved. It is more economic, therefore, to change large amounts infrequently, which rather defeats the security aspect of traveller's cheques. Passports must always be presented when changing traveller's cheques or using cards for obtaining cash. The questions asked vary according to the bank, but many still wish to know your address in Spain; if this is uncertain, just give the name of your last or any local hotel — no-one cares in any case. Eurocheques have the advantage of flexibility, but only a few banks accept them. In addition, the poor rates given and the various costs charged by the issuing banks make them an expensive proposition for obtaining cash. American Express and Thomas Cook will issue traveller's cheques in pesetas on request, usually giving a slightly better rate than for notes; unfortunately neither has a branch on Gran Canaria, which would change them free of charge. Until recently, Banco de Bilbao offered traveller's cheques in pesetas, which all their Spanish branches would exchange for notes without incurring costs, but this bank has merged with Banco de Vizcaya and no longer issues them. However, branches of Banco Bilbao-Vizcaya in major cities outside Spain will supply pesetas at a favourable rate, and free of charges. A certain amount of shopping around can be advantageous.

Most hotels, shops and restaurants accept traveller's cheques without charges, but few give a favourable rate, so traveller's cheques in pesetas are a better bet.

Major credit cards are widely accepted in the main resorts, and the conversion by credit card company is usually at a good rate, so this is often the best method of payment.

To summarize, use credit cards wherever possible, otherwise a combination of peseta notes and traveller's cheques in pesetas, with Eurocheques for emergencies, will prove to be the best combination for most holidaymakers.

Beaches & Watersports

Much of Gran Canaria's coastline is indented with beaches of some sort; most are of dark-grey volcanic sand, the golden sands of Playa del Inglés and Maspalomas are located in the south. Puerto Rico, on the south-west coast, also has golden sand, imported entirely from the Sahara.

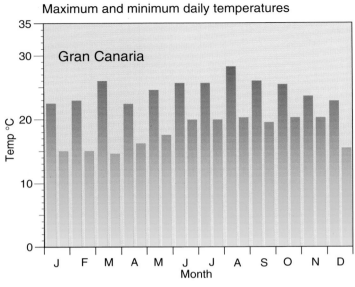

Maximum and minimum daily temperatures

Gran Canaria

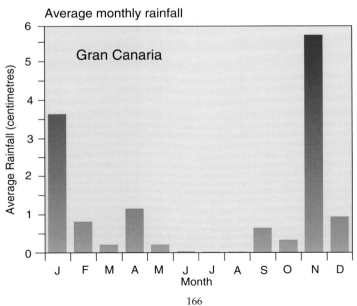

Average monthly rainfall

Gran Canaria

166

Due to currents and rock formations, some beaches are dangerous for swimmers; where this is the case, it is indicated in the text.

Strong winds blow almost perpetually on the south-east beaches, making them ideal for surfers and windsurfers. Sub-aqua enthusiasts are recommended to head for the more sheltered bays of the south-west coast, in particular that of Pasito Blanco.

Chemists

In Spain, chemists supply only pharmaceutical products, not toiletries or perfumes. A green cross and the word Farmacia generally signifies a chemists shop. Most close Saturday afternoons, Sundays and public holidays, but the name and address of the nearest chemist open will always be displayed.

Climate

The details of Gran Canaria's weather are discussed in the Introduction, while the average temperatures and rainfall are given in the charts. It is quite impossible to gauge the weather in Las Palmas visually from the southern resorts, as the skies above the city are hidden from them by the high mountains. Remember that cloud is affected by the mountains and wind direction, so that it may be cloudy or raining in the northern half of the island, while the south basks in glorious sunshine — when the wind, on rare occasions, switches to the south west the reverse situation can prevail.

Clothing

While Gran Canaria is never really cold at sea level, early mornings and evenings in winter can be cool enough to require a jacket or pullover to be worn. In the mountains, temperatures fall dramatically as the sun begins to sink or is obscured by cloud, and those planning a lengthy hike among them at any time of the year should take warm clothing — just in case. Nevertheless, unlike the islands of

Tenerife and La Palma, the mountains of Gran Canaria are not high enough for frost or snow to occur.

Most visitors will find that clothing in Gran Canaria is not particularly cheap, and are advised to bring sufficient summer-weight clothes with them. Only rarely will anything more that a tee-shirt or blouse, together with shorts or slacks — plus a bikini for the beach — be needed during the day in the sunny south, so do not overpack. Men intending to dine in smart hotels or attend a casino should bring a jacket and tie. Formal dress is never obligatory.

Duty Free Allowances

The Canaries are classed as being outside the European Union for customs purposes (due to a special arrangement) and therefore duty is applied to returning visitors as though they had been to a non-EU country. This means, at the time of writing, that only one bottle of spirits and 200 cigarettes, for example, can be brought back. However, many are surprised to learn that almost double the value of duty-free goods other than tobacco, wines and spirits and perfumes, may be brought back from countries outside the European Union than from those within it. This makes it possible to return from Gran Canaria with watches and audio and camera equipment, which would not otherwise be permitted. In 1995, the maximum sterling value allowance was £136, but if a single item exceeded that amount, the duty on its full value would have to be paid. It is not permitted for a group of people to pool their alllowances in order to purchase a duty-free item that exceeds £136 in value and bring it back without paying the full duty.

To assess the current situation, visitors from the United Kingdom should ask for *A Guide for Travellers*, issued by Customs and Excise at departure airports.

Electricity

Most electricity supply in Gran Canaria is 220-225AC; only in out-of-the- way villages or very old premises will 110-125AC be encountered. The usual continental two-point plugs are accepted, but they are just too small for the British equivalent and an adaptor, which can be purchased in the UK, will be needed.

Festivals & Special Events

The dates of many festivals are based on the variable Christian calendar and will change slightly each year. The exact dates may be found either from the Spanish National Tourist Office in advance, or on arrival in Gran Canaria. Some of the fiestas are described in the text.The venues indicated here are where the most important celebrations take place, but other festivals are also held on the island.

6 January
Las Palmas, Teror, Agüimes, Gáldar: Cabalgata de los Rey Magos (The three Kings Horseback Parade)

20 January
Tejeda and Valsequillo: Almond Blossom festival

February/March
Las Palmas: Opera Festival
Santa Catalina quarter of Las Palmas, Telde, Agüimes, San Agustín, Maspalmomas and Playa del Inglés: Carnaval. Carnaval in the southern resorts follows that of Las Palmas.

March/April
All the island: Semana Santa (Holy Week)

29 April
Fortaleza de Ansite, Las Palmas: Anniversary of Gran Canaria's incorporation into the Crown of Castile

May
Gáldar, Teror, San Nicolás: Fiesta de San Isidro

May/June
Las Palmas, Arucas: Corpus Christi

29 June
Las Palmas: Foundation of Las Palmas

6 July
Fataga: Fiesta del Albaricoque (apricots)

25 July
Gáldar, San Bartolomé de Tirajana: Feast Day of St James

(Santiago), who is the Patron Saint of Spain

4 August
Puerto de las Nieves and Agaete: Bajada de la Rama

8 September
Teror: Romería de la Virgen del Pino

10 September
Puerto de la Aldea: Fiesta del Charco

October (first Sunday)
Puerto de la Luz, Las Palmas: Fiesta de la Naval (celebrates the defeat of Sir Francis Drake's fleet in 1595 and may not, therefore, be of great appeal to chauvinistic British holiday-makers)

October
Agüimes: Fiesta de la Traide del Gofio y Agua (Festival of the Bringing of Maize and Water)

November
Teror: Fiesta del Rancho de Animas

December (first fortnight)
Santa Lucía, Arucas, Gáldar: Fiesta de la Luz (Festival of light)

31 December
Las Canteras Beach, Las Palmas: New Year's Eve celebrations

Food & Drink Vocabulary

Food and drink in Gran Canaria is described generally in the Introduction, but the glossary below will help to understand those menus which are not translated into English.

* against an entry denotes that it is a speciality of the Canaries.

Aceite	oil	Albóndigas	meat balls
Aceituna	olive	Alcachofas	artichokes
Aguacate	avocado pear	Almendras	almonds
Ahumada	smoked	Anchoas	anchovies
Ajillo	garlic	Arroz	rice
Ajo	garlic	Atún	tunny

170

Azafrán	saffron rice		made with
Bacalao	dried, salted cod		chillis, and then very fiery
Baifo*	kid braised in a piquant sauce	Chuletas	chops
		Churros	fried batter in thin tubes, a popular
Berenjena	aubergine		
Bienmesabes*	a sweet confection of honey, eggs and almonds		breakfast snack
		Cocido Canario*	a thick stew, made with local vegetables (also known as *puchero*)
Bistec	steak		
Bocadillo	sandwich		
Boquerónes	fresh anchovies		
Burgado	winkles	Conejo	rabbit
Caballa	mackerel	Cordero	lamb
Cabrito	kid	Cordoníz	quail
Calabacín	courgette	Dátil	date
Calamares	squid	Durazno	peach (*melocotón* also, as on the mainland)
Caldo de pescado	fish soup		
Camarones	tiny shrimps		
Carne	meat	Ensalada	salad (*variata* — mixed, *verde* or *sin tomates* — green)
Cazuela*	fish stew with potatoes and saffron		
Cebolla	onion		
Cebolla boba*	pickled onion	Entremeses	hors d'oeuvre
		Escaldón*	juice from a *cazuela* fish stew with *gofio* added
Cerdo	pork		
Champiñon	mushroom		
Cherne*	a local coarse-textured fish, frequently salted		
		Estofado	braised
		Faisán	pheasant
		Filete	fillet (meat)
Chipirones	baby squid	Flan	crème caramel
Chorizo	spicy sausage, eaten cold or hot in stews: sometimes		
		Fresa	strawberry
		Frio	cold
		Frito	fried

Garbanzo compuesto*	chick-pea and potato stew with *gofio*		and correctly, known as *Pata de Cerdo*
Galletas de almendra*	almond biscuits	Jamón serrano	lean, dry-cured ham
Gazpacho	iced soup: usually of tomato, cucumber, olive oil, vinegar, garlic, pimento and croutons	Judías	beans
		Lapa	clam
		Leche	milk
		Lechón	suckling pig
		Lechuga	lettuce
		Legumbres	vegetables
		Lima	lime
		Limón	lemon
		Lomo	loin
Gofio*	toasted flour, traditionally ground maize	Manchego	ewe's-milk cheese from mainland Spain: varies in strength and texture with age
Guarnición	garnished		
Guisado	stewed		
Guisantes	peas		
Hamburguesa	hamburger		
Helado	ice-cream	Mantequilla	butter
Higado	liver	Manzana	apple
Higos	fig	Mariscos	seafood
Horno(al)	baked	Matalahuva*	cumin-flavoured bread
Huevos	eggs		
duro	— hard		
escalfado	— poached	Mejillones	mussels
frito	— fried	Merluza	hake
revuelto	— scrambled	Miel	honey
Ibérico	mountain breed of pig	Miel de palma*	honey made from the sap of the palm tree — a speciality of the island of La Palma
Jamón	ham		
Jamón Canario*	cold leg of roast pork, served with hot *papas arrugadas* and *mojo picón*. More commonly,		
		Morcilla	spicy black pudding
		Mojo*	sauces, usually served cold,

	made with a base of oil, vinegar, garlic and salt. *Mojo picón*, a fiery red version, which incorporates pimentos, is the most popular. *Mojo verde*'s green colour comes from the addition of fresh coriander leaves. Both may be obtained, bottled, in supermarkets
Mostaza	mustard
Names	yams (sweet potatoes)
Naranja	orange
Nata	whipped cream
Paella	saffron rice, cooked with fish, chicken, shellfish and vegetables
Pan	bread
Papas arrugadas*	very small Canary potatoes, boiled in salt water and served in their jackets: hence, *arrugadas* (wrinkled); usually accompanied by *mojo picón*.
Papas turradas*	Canary potatoes roasted or grilled
Papas viudas*	roast potatoes with ham and vegetables
Papaya	an oval fruit with orange flesh, also known in English as paw paw; often eaten for breakfast sprinkled with fresh lime juice, when it is accredited with aphrodisiac properties.
Parilla (a la)	grilled
Parillada criollo	charcoal-grilled steak
Pasas	raisins
Pastas	biscuits
Pastel	cake
Pata de cerdo*	cold roast leg of pork, sometimes also called, incorrectly, *jamón Canario*

Pato	duck
Pepino	cucumber
Pepito	long sandwich
Pera-melón*	pear-melon, a locally grown fruit
Perdíz	partridge
Pescado	fish
Pez espada	swordfish
Pimienta	pepper
Piñas asadas	corn on the cob
Pinchito	kebab
Plancha (a la)	grilled on a hot plate
Plátano	banana
Plátanos Canarias*	bananas cooked in brandy
Platos combinados	dish of several components at an inclusive price
Pollo	chicken
Pollo asado	roast chicken
Postres	desserts
Potaje	dish
Potaje de berros*	watercress soup
Puchero*	a thick stew, as *cocido*
Pulpo	octopus
Quesadilla*	cheesecake from the island of Hierro
Queso	cheese
Queso de flor*	goat's milk cheese flavoured with flowers from the cardoom thistle: made in Guía
Rancho Canario*	thick vegetable soup with *gofio* and sometimes pork
Rapaduras*	confection of honey and almonds from La Palma island
Riñones	kidneys
Ropa vieja*	literally 'old clothes', a dish of left-overs, mainly found in *tapas* bars
Sal	salt
Salchichón	hard, salami-type sausage, eaten cold
Salmonete	red mullet
Salsa	sauce
Sancocho*	fish, usually salted cherne, poached with potatoes. *Mojo picón* and dried fruit or a sweet fudge based on *gofio* is served with the dish. *Sancocho* is popular for Sunday lunch

Sobrasada	type of *chorizo* spread (from Majorca)		the Christmas period, made□ in the shape of small fish, hence the name, meaning 'Christmas trout'.
Solo	on its own		
Solomillo	sirloin steak		
Sopa	soup		
Sopa de ajo	soup of garlic, paprika, bread and an egg yolk		
Ternera	veal	Turrón*	chewy confection of honey and *gofio*
Tortilla	plain omelette		
Tortilla Española	'Spanish' omelette, with onions and potatoes, firn textured, eaten hot or cold	Vapor (al)	steamed
		Vieja*	local fish with a lobster-like texture, hard to find in winter
Truchas navideñas*	pastries filled with almonds, yams and pumpkin, which are available in	Vinagre	vinegar
		Yema	egg yolk
		Zumo de fruta	fruit juice

Restaurant Queries & Requests

Ashtray	cenicero	Cup	taza
Beer	cerveza	Drinks	bebidas
Bill	cuenta	Dry	seco
Bread	pan	Fork	tenedor
Butter	mantequilla	Glass (for water or beer)	vaso
Cheese	queso		
Coffee — black	café solo		
Coffee — white	café con leche	Glass (for wine)	copa
Cold	frio	Hot (temperature)	caliente
Cream	nata		
Credit card	tarjeta de credito	Hot (flavour)	picante
		Ice	hielo

Ice-cream	helados	Serviette	servilleta
Knife	cuchillo	Set menu	menu del día
Lime	lima	Speciality	especialidad
Less	menor	Spoon	cuchara
Lemon	limón	Sugar	azúcar
Medium	regular or mediano	Sweet	dulce
		Tea	té
Menu	carta	Thank you	gracias
More	más	Traveller's cheques	cheques de viajes
Mustard	mostaza		
Neat (on its own)	solo	Vinegar	vinagre
		Waiter	camarero
Nothing	nada	Water (tap)	agua corriente (or del grifo)
Oil	aceite		
Pepper (condiment)	pimienta	Water (gassy mineral)	agua con gas
Plate	plato	Water (flat mineral)	agua sin gas
Please	por favor		
Rare	poco hecho	Well done	muy (or bien) hecho
Roll	panecillo		
Salad	ensalada	Wine (white)	vino blanco
Salt	sal	Wine (red)	vino tinto
Sandwich	bocadillo	Wine (rose)	vino rosado

Health

As Gran Canaria is a member of the European Union, free health facilities are available to visitors from other countries within the union — an EIII form must be obtained from a Post Office before departure. However, private health insurance is still advisable to ensure prompt attention. No particular health problems are posed in Gran Canaria, apart from the possibility of 'Spanish tummy' for those not used to continental food, or an excess of alcohol. Is is always advisable to bring a supply of products such as Immodium on holiday so that immediate self treatment is available. Should problems persist, the local chemist will be able to supply a specific remedy, including antibiotics if necessary, without a doctor's prescription.

Language

Castillian Spanish is spoken throughout the island but, unlike peninsular Spaniards, Canarios never lisp the letters c or z, and they often omit to pronounce the letter s. The lilting manner of speaking is reminiscent of South American countries, and so are some of the words used, eg *guagua* for bus, rather than *autobus* and *papas* for potatoes, rather than *patates*. An accent above a vowel indicates where the stress should be placed; a wiggly line above an 'n' (ñ) means a 'ny' sound rather than an 'n' sound, eg the country's name (España) is pronounced 'Espanya', not 'A spanner'.

Many Canarios, particularly those working in the tourist industry, now speak English.

Maps

The maps printed in this book highlight the location of places of visitor interest, but a large scale road map is recommended for motoring. A good scale map of the island is issued by the tourist board free of charge, however some destinations are not pinpointed accurately enough. Firestone also publish a map of the island, which is somewhat clearer to follow, albeit to a smaller scale. The main drawback to this is that, at the time of writing, the map of Las Palmas, which is included, is out of date and inaccurate with regard to street names. A map published by Manuel Brito Auyanet is quite easy to follow and widely available on the island.

Most published street plans of Las Palmas, due to the shape of the city, are orientated east/west, rather than the usual north/south, which can be confusing.

Measurements

As may be expected, the metric system is used exclusively. When shopping, it is helpful to remember that 100 grams is slightly less that ¼lb and 1 kilogram is slightly more than 2lb. A kilometre measures between ½ and ¾ of a mile. There are almost precisely 8km to 5 miles.

Motoring

Many will wish to hire a car for at least part of the holiday. A national driving licence for any EU country is valid throughout Spain, but UK visitors must also produce their passports for identification. Virtually all hire companies accept major credit cards, which are the simplest method of payment, and avoid the otherwise obligatory deposit that is required. Local tax is added to the final bill. Due to the small size of the island, most hire companies do not charge a distance supplement — but check. Also check if driving on unsurfaced roads is forbidden by the hire company. The holidaymaker's travel insurance may already cover against accident — if not, take comprehensive insurance. The names of every person that may possibly drive the car should be included on the agreement. Ensure that all the vehicles controls are understood and in working order, and obtain a 24-hour contact telephone number.

Do not leave anything in parked cars (see Security).

Driving, of course, is on the right, and precedence must be given to other drivers approaching from the right at junctions or roundabouts. Vehicles must never be parked on a single line, nor must they face oncoming traffic. Speed limits are currently: built-up zones 40km/hr, dual carriageways (*carreteras*) 90km/hr, and the motorway (*autopista*) 120km/hr, and these must be strictly observed in order to avoid confrontation with the traffic police (Guardia Civil). Parking facilities are indicated by 'Aparcamiento', no parking by 'Estacionamiento Prohibido'. 'Cedo el Paso' means give right of way.

Most service stations are closed on Sundays.

Main roads in Gran Canaria are given a C prefix, except the *autopista*, which is called GC1, and minor roads that are surfaced also numbered, eg 6.1. Unfortunately for motorists who are not familiar with the island, road numbers, all too frequently, are not indicated.

The Canarios do not, in general, drive as aggressively as their mainland counterparts. If you are not in an hurry, let locals pass wherever it is safe to do so.

Museums

There are few museums in Gran Canaria, and most are concentrated in the Vegueta quarter of Las Palmas. Rarely is an entry charge made, with the notable exception of the Museo de Arte Sacro, which has to be entered in order to tour the interior of the cathedral.

Postage

Most who have spent a holiday in Gran Canaria will return home long before their postcard to the next-door-neighbour has arrived. To avoid this, bring pre-typed, addressed brown envelopes which will take the usual postcard size, and insert the card thereby fooling the 'system', which judges tourist postcards to be extremely non-urgent mail. When purchasing a card also buy a stamp at the same venue, or at a tobacconists as a last resort. Never go to a Post Office (*Correo*) just for stamps — the queues can be horrendous.

Public Holidays

1 January	New Year's Day
6 January	Epiphany
February/March	Shrove Tuesday (Las Palmas)
19 March	Feast of San José (St Joseph)
March/April	Maundy Thursday
	Good Friday
1 May	Labour Day
May	Corpus Christi Day
	Ascension Day
29 June	Feast Day of San Pedro and San Pablo
18 July	National Day
25 July	Feast Day of St James (Santiago)
15 August	Assumption Day
12 October	Día de la Hispanidad (Discovery of America Day)
1 November	All Saints Day

6 December	National Constitution Day
8 December	Feast Day of the Immaculate Conception of Mary
25 December	Christmas Day

Radio

Local broadcasts in English are particularly useful for weather forecasts and special events in Gran Canaria. Check the wavebands and programme times on arrival. The BBC World Service can also be heard on shortwave, and occasionally, at night, BBC Radio 4 can be recieved, particularly in Las Palmas.

Security

Visitors should be security conscious at all times. While crime is not a major problem, tourists — in particular those with hire cars — are the targets for petty theft. The editor of this book had his hire car broken into three times in three days and even a wheel was stolen! While the greatest risk is in the capital and the large resorts, small towns are not immune. Try to park where illegal activity will be more easily noticed, and do not leave *anything* in the car, even in the boot. If possible, remove the hire company's name stickers, which just advertise the fact that the car is being used by a tourist.

The usual sensible precautions against pick-pockets should be taken.

Shopping

Low taxes and no duty permit shopkeepers in Gran Canaria to charge relatively low prices for luxury items, particularly watches, cameras and audio equipment. It is essential, however, to obtain an internationally-valid guarantee, and to buy only from a reputable shop; it is also important to know in advance the lowest price that is being asked for the same item in duty-free shops at departure airports, and even, in some cases, in the high street at home. Not everything is a bargain — and bear in mind the £136 limit permitted by Customs and Excise.

Alcoholic drinks in litre bottles and cigarettes (by the carton) are best purchased in large *supermercados* (super-markets), the further away from tourist areas the better. Canary souvenirs of quality include embroidery — but watch out for fake imports — palm-leaf baskets, and knives and boxes made of bone with inlay metalwork. Cigar lovers should try Palmitos cigars, which come from the island of La Palma, and Miel de Palma palm tree honey, from the same island. Shops open generally 9am-1pm and 4-7pm, although the large department stores forego the afternoon siesta.

Telephones

A service charge is levied by hotels for making calls from rooms. Many public kiosks, usually painted yellow and displaying the word *Teléfono*, may be used for international calls. Remember to check if there is a time difference involved. To make a call anywhere in the United Kingdom, dial 07, pause for the tone, followed by 353 and the local code, but omitting the initial 0, and then the number.

For Eire, dial 07 followed by 44; once again omit the initial 0 of the local code and then ring the number.

Time

At the time of writting, unlike mainland Spain, but like the United Kingdom, The Canary Islands follow Greenwich Mean Time in winter, and are one hour ahead of it in summer.

Time-Share Touts

It is difficult to avoid time-share touts in the main tourist resorts, nevertheless a firm but polite 'No thank you' should deter all but the most persistent (unless of course you actually *want* a time share, or are willing to endure a lengthy sales presentation). English-speaking visitors to

Playa del Inglés are less likely to be pestered by the German-speaking touts (although as most are young students their English is often quite good), whereas in Puerto Rico the touts are English.

Do not be fooled by scratch-card competitions for free holidays, which you will invariably 'win'. Although the touts claim represent some official-sounding all-Canaries tourist organisation that has nothing to do with time-shares (and they even have official-looking identity cards), the 'winners' have to visit the local office to collect their 'prize', where they will be subjected to a time-share sales presentation.

Tipping

A service charge is included in most bills, and no additional gratuity is expected: this includes all hotel and restaurant bills and taxi fares. However, for good personal service a small tip is appreciated.

Toilet Facilities

Public toilets are virtually non-existent in Gran Canaria, apart from the airport and the Estación de Guaguas in Las Palmas. However, no bars, restaurants or hotels may, by law, refuse the use of their facilities to anyone, including non-customers. General terms denoting toilets are: *servicios*, *lavabos* and *aseos*; *señores* or *caballeros* denote men's toilets, and *señoras* or *señyoretes* women's toilets. Signs rather than words are used on occasions — do not confuse the woman making up her lips with the man smoking his pipe — both are quite similar.

Tourist Information Offices

Spanish Tourist Board Offices

UK
57-58 St James's Street
London SW1A 1LD
☎ 0171 499 0901

USA
665 5th Avenue
New York, NY10017
☎ 212 759 8822

845 N Michigan Avenue
Chicago
Illinois 60611
☎ 312 944 0215

Canada
60 Bloor Street West
Suite 201
Toronto
Ontario M4W 3B8
☎ 416 961 3131

Tourist Offices in Gran Canaria

Yumbo Centrum
Playa del Inglés
☎ 76 78 48
Open: Monday-Friday 9am-2pm, 3-9pm (closes at 8pm in summer), Saturday 9am-3pm

Gando Airport
Open: Monday-Friday
9.30am-3pm

Parque de Santa Catalina
Las Palmas
☎ 26 46 23
Open: Monday-Friday 9am-2pm

Transport (Public)

Buses
Not all holidaymakers to Gran Canaria opt to hire a car for all, or even part of their stay, but many will wish to explore the island without having to resort to coach excursions. They are well catered for by the local bus services, which link virtually every part of Gran Canaria, no matter how remote.

Throughout this book, most numbers of the buses that follow the itineraries described have been given; only rarely, however, are specific departure times shown, because this would be too cumbersome and, more important, they are liable to change. It is recommended that a choice of the itineraries that appeal is made at an early stage, and the numbers of the relevant buses noted. Timetable cards for each one can then be requested, which will give most of the information needed.

Those staying in the south can obtain travel information and timetable cards at the Yumbo Centrum in Playa del

Inglés, either from the Tourist Information Office or the adjacent Salcai Office (for the southern routes, all of which they operate). If it soon becomes apparent that a route will be followed repeatedly, eg San Agustín to Faro de Maspalomas, a ticket valid for ten journeys can be purchased from Salcai at a much reduced price.

Salcai buses, painted green and white, are the only public services operating in the south, other buses, eg Las Palmas Bus and Maspalomas Bus are for private hire only. Bus stops are indicated by a sign with a blue circle surrounded by a red line, and bearing a red diagonal stripe, the word bus and a large P (for *Parada*) will be displayed. Confusingly, many bus stops in the south bear a Palmitos Park Bus Stop sign; while buses to Palmitos Park do stop at them, so also do buses on other routes.

All Salcai buses to Las Palmas terminate at the subterranean Estación de Guaguas, facing Parque de San Telmo. From here also operate the Utinsa buses, painted blue and orange, which serve the north of the island, and depart from a separate group of bays. Information and timetables for both Salcai and Utinsa buses can be obtained from their respective offices located here.

From the Salcai office, Bono Guagua tickets may be purchased, which are valid for ten journeys on buses covering the metropolitan area of Las Palmas; run by Guaguas Municipales, they are painted yellow. It is necessary to ascend the stairs or ramp from the bus station to Parque de San Telmo for the municipal bus stops.

Many other outlets also sell Bono Guagua tickets in Las Palmas, including most banks, several tobacconists, and all the branches of Despacho 1x2. A half price Salcai return ticket from Las Palmas to the southern resorts is available on Sundays and public holidays — but not in the reverse direction.

Bonobus tickets must be inserted in the cancelling machine on the bus. Single tickets (one way, never return) are purchased on the vehicle, which is entered from the front and vacated from the rear. It will help to follow a map, in case the bus driver forgets the destination requested. Most buses have a red button, which should be pushed to halt the bus. At bus stops, raise an arm to halt a bus.

Tartanas
These horse-drawn open carriages, operating only in Las Palmas, can hardly be termed public transport, but they offer a leisurely, if expensive, way of seeing the city. Up to four people can be seated in a *tartana*, and the price charged is for the vehicle, not per person. A regular pick-up point is the Hotel Santa Catalina, in Parque Doramas, and the Parque de Santa Catalina area. Tariffs appear to be negotiable.

Taxis
No duty and low tax once meant cheap taxi fares throughout the Canaries but, sadly, this is no longer the case. It is important for most visitors, therefore, to become acquainted with the buses as soon as possible. In Las Palmas fares are always metered, but in other locations they are sometimes not — negotiate in advance: all taxi drivers must carry a fares chart in their cab. A *libre* sign denotes that the taxi is free; at night, this is supplemented by a green light.

Water

Tap water, although safe in most tourist areas and Las Palmas, is almost never drunk in Gran Canaria. Mineral water, flat (*sin gas*) or fizzy (*con gas*), is readily available. It is cheaper purchased in litre bottle size, or even larger, from supermarkets, although the relatively expensive smaller sizes can be useful for the beach. Firgas, bottled from a spring in Gran Canaria, is the most popular brand throughout the Canary Islands.

Index

Visitor's Guides

Itinerary based guides for independent travellers

MPC

America:
American South West
California
Florida
Massachusetts, Rhode
    Island & Connecticut
Orlando & C Florida
USA
Vermont, New Hamp-
    shire & Maine

Austria:
Austria
Austria: Tyrol &
    Vorarlberg

Britain:
Cornwall & Isles of
    Scilly
Cotswolds
Devon
East Anglia
Hampshire & Isle of
    Wight
Kent
Lake District
Scotland
Somerset, Dorset &
    Wiltshire
N Wales & Snowdonia
North York Moors,
    York & Coast
Northern Ireland
Peak District
Treasure Houses of
    England
Yorkshire Dales &
    North Pennines

Bruges
Canada
Cuba
Czech & Slovak
    Republics

Denmark
Egypt

France:
Champagne &
    Alsace-Lorraine
France
Alps & Jura
Brittany
Burgundy &
    Beaujolais
Dordogne
Gascony & Midi
    Pyrenees
Loire
Massif Central
Normandy
Normandy Landing
    Beaches
Provence & Côte d'Azur
Vendee & Poitou-
    Charentes

Germany:
Bavaria
Black Forest
Northern Germany
Rhine & Mosel
Southern Germany

Greece:
Greece (mainland)
Athens &
    Peloponnese

Holland
Hungary
Iceland & Greenland

India:
Delhi, Agra & Rajasthan
Goa

Islands:
Corsica
Crete
Cyprus
Gran Canaria
Guernsey, Alderney &
    Sark
Jamaica
Jersey
Madeira
Mallorca, Menorca,
    Ibiza & Formentera
Malta & Gozo
Mauritius, Rodrigues
    & Reunion
Rhodes
Sardinia
Seychelles
Sri Lanka
Tenerife
Windward Islands

Italy:
Florence & Tuscany
Italian Lakes
Northern Italy
Southern Italy

New Zealand
Norway
Portugal

Spain:
Costa Brava
    & Costa Blanca
Northern & Central
    Spain
Southern Spain
    & Costa del Sol

South Africa
Sweden
Switzerland
Thailand
Turkey

MPC Visitor's Guides are available through all good bookshops. In case of local difficulty, you may order direct (quoting Visa / Access number) from Grantham Book Services on ☎ 01476 67421. Ask for the cash sales department. There is a small charge for postage and packing.